Branding Basics for Small Business

How to Create an Irresistible Brand on Any Budget

Maria Ross

Branding Basics for Small Business Rides a Wave of Praise

Maria Ross cuts through the fluff and explains why strong brands are built on customers' experiences, and not on huge advertising budgets. Complete with real examples from top companies, this book is a roadmap leading small businesses and entrepreneurs in the right direction.

Adam Sutton,
MarketingSherpa.com

....

(This book) is a wise and recommended read, not to be missed by any small business.

Midwest Book Review

....

In today's social economy, every business is a brand, regardless of size. And when Ross states that every new hire is a brand ambassador, she proves unequivocally that she 'gets it'. The question small business owners must ask is if they want to be the ones controlling that brand or the ones left to salvage it. In this book, you'll learn how to nail down your brand before you spend valuable resources. Your brand is more than just a logo. It's everything you are and the ticket to positive ROI.

Lisa Barone, Chief Branding Officer,
Outspoken Media

....

You've got such a wide and clear scope on what makes successful brands so ... successful. Great coverage. And great inspiration to be true to your values and think big.

Danielle LaPorte, lead author of
Style Statement: Live by Your Own Design
and the upcoming *Firestarter Sessions;*
creator of *WhiteHotTruth.com*

As someone who has worked with thousands of small businesses, I have seen a lack of a clear, focused brand strategy cause people to waste time, energy, money and flounder in the marketplace. Never fear, Maria breaks down branding so that anyone with a business, or who is thinking of launching a business, can understand why an investment in branding is make or break for creating a thriving business. Don't launch without it!

Beth Schoenfeldt,
Co-Founder, Collective-E,
an Entrepreneur's Agency and Community

NorLightsPress.com
762 State Road 458
Bedford IN 47421

Printed in the United States of America
ISBN: 978-1-935254-24-9

Cover Design by Bridget Perez, TRAY Creative
(www.traycreative.com)

Book Design by Nadene Carter

Second printing, 2011

For Paul

Contents

Introduction 1

Part 1: What Is Brand and Why Does It Matter? . . . 5

What Is a Brand?. 5

Brand Identity Crisis 11

Branding Myths Shattered 12

Branding vs. PR vs. Marketing vs.
Social Media...Oh My! 17

Branding and Marketing Are Not the Same 18

Branding Is Not Public Relations 20

Branding Is Not Social Media 23

Why Does Brand Matter? 27

What's Your Reason for Being? 28

Building a Brand That Can Change
with the Times 30

Rabid Fans: Your Logo Should be My Tattoo 33

Don't Leave it to Chance: People Will Form
Their Own Brand Impressions 34

How to Avoid Random Acts of Marketing:
Brand Strategy as Your Foundation 38

Brand as Investment Guidepost. 40

Brand as Asset 44

Brand as Competitive Weapon 45

All Markets Have a Brand Need: Proud to be
Cheap and Disposable 51

Brand is Not Just a Logo: It's Everything 54

Brand as Design Guide: Hug a Designer Today 56

Part 2: How to Build Your Brand Strategy 59

Ten Key Questions to Building Your
Brand Strategy 60

Part 3: Applying the Brand Strategy 97

Brand Building Blocks: Choosing a Name 99

Brand Building Blocks: Creating Your
Visual Identity System 104

Brand Building Blocks: Crafting
Your Key Messages 109

Use Brand to Guide Your Marketing Investments . . . 126

The Rule of Three 129

Operationalizing Your Brand 133

Little Things Mean a Lot: Find Unique
Ways to Delight Your Customers 137

Hire Well: Every New Hire is a
Brand Ambassador 142

When to Rebrand 147

Everything Stems From Brand 155

About the Author 157

Acknowledgements 159

Introduction

Why Small Business Owners and Start-ups Need This Book

EVERY DAY OF OUR LIVES we're forced to endure bad marketing. Today, we humans create and assimilate a barrage of corporate messages and images that was unheard of a century ago. The noise gets louder as companies fight to rise above the crowd. The moment they find a new way to do this, the tactic is abused and destroyed until it breaks down and the next new thing arrives to take its place.

I've had enough. I want to start a brand revolution.

I admit it: during my marketing, advertising, and branding career, I've been guilty of adding to the scrap pile. That was simply because we were not always operating from a strong brand foundation and were just chasing the next new thing. I have since learned that when a strong Brand Strategy is created first and then executed clearly and consistently – even in the most subtle ways – it can pack a huge punch.

Why do some companies delight us so much? And if we must be inundated with all these marketing messages in today's world, why can't we expect, nay, demand, more *delight*?

Effective advertising and messaging stem from strong branding. Without a strong Brand Strategy, organizations flounder, trying out different marketing tactics in order to find one that sticks.

In a way, good branding is an art form, and like any art it has the power to inspire, delight, anger, provoke, motivate, and entertain. Good branding can transform a frumpy housewife into a triathlete (Nike), an average guy into a chick magnet (Axe), a plain Jane into graceful royalty (Tiffany), a take-out food junkie into a dinner party diva (Williams Sonoma), or a simple accountant into a rebellious road warrior (Harley Davidson). It can even inspire us to get involved in our communities and take an active interest in government (Obama).

This ability to inspire and delight has finally been discovered in the non-profit arena to great success. Non-profits like the ASPCA are realizing that the secret sauce that makes a for-profits' balance sheet look so good can also apply to their image, message, and brand. I've been lucky enough to work with non-profits through volunteer organizations such as the Taproot Foundation (www.taprootfoundation.org) and affectionately term this "using brand for good rather than evil."

A strong brand that connects with the subconscious and emotional reasons why donors give to charity can get money pouring through the doors. The APSCA's message and brand spurs millions to open their wallets for the benefit of animals. And guess what? For many non-profits, the compelling benefit isn't necessarily making the world a better place; sometimes it's tapping into a donor's desire to simply feel good about themselves.

I've always had a personal mission to create brands that change the world. I seek to do this with every client, even if they only reach one person a day. I believe organizations of all sizes can create brands that delight, inspire, and make the world a better place – in big or small ways – while still making stockholders or owners happy.

I believe simple, well-crafted, well-targeted brand messages can accomplish more with less. We've seen hundreds of examples of companies like Apple, Virgin, and Starbucks that built their strong, simple brands early and now attract new fans, expand into new business lines, and increase sales – seemingly without effort. And yet, so many other companies chase the next best thing to get their message heard above the din.

Small business owners often wish they could emulate the big guys, even if those guys aren't doing things well. They carry the added burden of trying to do everything themselves, from scratch, and often forsake branding in their quest to get immediate sales and keep the doors open another month. Who can blame them when one person has to be Chief Officer, Accountant, Operations Manager, Marketing Manager, and in many cases, the actual producer of the goods and services they sell? When you're knee-deep in inventory control, invoicing, lease agreements, or supplier quality control, branding can seem like an afterthought, or a luxury you can't afford.

My goal with this book is to help small businesses, startups, and even non-profit organizations build meaningful brands that *connect* with their audiences: Brands that say something about their customers and partners, extend easily into other products or services, and turn customers and partners into evangelists. They can learn these lessons by emulating large, successful companies as well as businesses right around the corner.

I'd love to see more marketing out there that doesn't insult our intelligence, waste our time, or offend our senses. I want to show you how everyone in the organization influences brand and how a complete Brand Strategy now will help you make a thousand little decisions later on, so you can reap big rewards, get that cash register to ring, appeal to new donors, and attract rabid, loyal fans.

Enjoy the ride. It'll be fun.

Part 1:
What Is Brand and Why Does It Matter?

What Is a Brand?

IN THE MID-1990s, NIKE introduced a branding and advertising campaign called *If You Let Me Play*. The ad campaign was an offshoot of their iconic *Just Do It* message. The ads showed poignant close-ups of young girls of every race saying,

If you let me play sports
I will like myself more;
I will have more self-confidence,
If you let me play sports.
If you let me play,
I will be 60 percent less likely to get breast cancer;
I will suffer less depression.
If you let me play sports,
I will be more likely to leave a man who beats me.
If you let me play,
I will be less likely to get pregnant before I want to.
I will learn what it means to be strong.
If you let me play sports.
If you let me play sports.*

---

*Ashley Koehn, *"The Power of Team,"* http://inside.nike.com/blogs/
nikewomenen_US/2009/04/27/the-power-of-team (April 27, 2009)

From a pure business perspective, Nike designed this ad to sell apparel and accessories to women. Their campaign struck a powerful chord and hit me on a visceral level, making me see Nike in a whole new light.

I admired how the message went beyond "buy our stuff." This campaign was about empowering our girls, strengthening them, saving them from abuse and self-doubt, and putting them on a healthy path to adulthood. The ad was about equality, opportunity, and challenging yourself. As I looked into the eyes of the young girls on TV, I fell in love with Nike. I wanted to support Nike and all its efforts. Despite the controversies Nike has faced over the years, I smile when I recall that campaign. I hope it saved at least one girl by giving her courage and hope.

Nike showed me that a business can have a mission-driven brand and still make money. But what is this mysterious thing called brand and why should we care?

Brand is your story, your core purpose, and your customer promise. Brand is your reputation – which ultimately lives in the minds of your customers. Brand is what your customers say it is, not what you say it is, but you can shape and influence it through intentional decisions and actions. A clear, consistent brand will shape your business, guide your investments, and help you grow and prosper. And regardless of budget crunches or time constraints, your small business, non-profit, or startup can build a strong brand just like Nike. You have a powerful story to tell and a mission to accomplish. With your advantage of being small and much closer to the customer than global corporations, you have the power to engage and inspire your audience, however large it is, and make your community or world a better place.

Think about the big guys like Nike, Disney, Virgin, and Apple. How does reading the names of these companies make you feel? What images immediately come to mind? What emotions do they evoke?

Recall a memorable shopping experience you've had. How did you respond to the store, the clerk's competence, and his behavior toward you? Was the store layout appealing or did you feel anxious, claustrophobic, and manic? How did you feel about yourself when you left the store carrying their bag? Did you feel happier, smarter, more sophisticated, and more eco-savvy – or were you embarrassed to carry the store's logo around?

That, ladies and gentlemen, is brand in action.

But what does brand truly mean?

Some people believe brand is merely a logo, a website, or company colors. I work with many business owners who say, "Oh, I don't need a Brand Strategy. I already have my logo and business cards, thank you." But those items are only outer symbols of the brand – vehicles that communicate your brand to the world. They are not the brand itself.

For years, Scott Montgomery, a creative director and agency principal for Bradley and Montgomery Advertising (www.bamideas.com), has been building and communicating brands in unique ways for the likes of Microsoft, VH-1 and Chase Bank. He also lectures frequently on branding and has been featured on NPR and in *The New York Times*. Here's what Scott has to say about brand:

> "In a world where absolutely everything in media is changing, let me try to define "brand" in a way that won't. A brand is exactly two things: It's the promise your offering makes to people, and the clothes that promise is dressed in. The degree to which that combination generates the behavior you want from people is all that matters. "

Brand is the core experience, the story, and the essence of your business. It's your company's reputation, personality, and reason for being – all rolled into one package.

Brand contains the promise you make to customers, the value your product or services provide, and the difference between you and your competition. Brand is your reputation, your image, and the "mind share" you occupy in people's brains based on their experiences with you, whether real or imagined.

Brand can also encompass your philosophy, a cause, and the reason you do what you do. You might think of brand as the personality and soul of an organization communicated in various ways, such as through a logo. Wikipedia says:

> 66 A brand is a collection of images and ideas representing an economic producer. Brand recognition and other reactions are created by the accumulation of experiences with the specific product or service, both directly relating to its use, and through the influence of advertising, design, and media commentary. A brand is a symbolic embodiment of all the information connected to a company, product or service. A brand serves to create associations and expectations among products made by a producer. 99

In this definition, I especially like the phrase: *both directly relating to its use, and through the influence of advertising, design, and media commentary*. This shows us that the brand experience you create is a two-way interaction across multiple vehicles. Your brand goes beyond the advertising or promotion you push out to customers. It's also based on people's first-hand interactions with your organization.

Brand communication is like a three-legged stool: it is expressed not only *visually* (in your logo, design, or colors), but *verbally* (in the words you use or copy you write), and *experientially* as well. An ad may tell me your company is fun, convenient, and easy to do business with, but if your clerks don't smile at me or your online checkout process is akin to taking a college entrance exam, then I'm going to doubt those brand promises.

Since brand is a promise, a reputation, and an actual experience, entities besides businesses can have a brand. For example, countries and cities have brands. What feeling do you get when you hear Paris, France versus Omaha, Nebraska? How about Antarctica versus Puerto Rico? I recently heard China is launching a rebranding effort to change their image on the world stage. Chinese authorities are going to highlight their scenic areas, corporate visitor centers, and museums in an effort to make the country seem more modern and welcoming.

In an article for *CorpComms Magazine,* Alfredo Muccino, the Chief Creative Officer of Liquid Agency (a branding firm in Silicon Valley), explained that London's brand is no longer the quaint "royal family/tea and crumpets" deal or the

"British punk movement." He feels England has morphed into something more cosmopolitan, blending the old and the new in a unique way.[1]

Events and holidays also have brands that evoke images and emotions. Take Christmas, for example. Many of us envision gathering with family and friends, decorating a tree, exchanging gifts, eating too much, and playing games with the kids. For some, Christmas has a warm, loving feeling attached to that brand. But since brand is defined by our own experiences, others may have a quite different take: to them, the brand of Christmas may represent chaos, budget woes, or stress. The brand is your own reality and experience of that event.

People may have their own brands, from politicians to movie stars. Famous personalities know the brand must be protected at all costs, which is why they're upset when photos are used without permission. Oprah's brand is a Midas touch for the books, people, and products she endorses. She zealously guards her media properties to protect her personal brand. No one besides Oprah appears on the cover of *O Magazine,* and her brand communicates exactly what she intends it to communicate.

We've all seen what can happen when a personal brand is tarnished, as with Tiger Woods and John Edwards. Once a brand goes bad, it's difficult to recover from the damage.

[1] CorpComms Magazine, *"Making London Hip Again,"* www.corp commsmagazine.co.uk, (October 6, 2009)

Brand Identity Crisis

Do you ever feel frustrated when a company brags about great customer service, then traps you for 35 minutes on a call center help line from hell? Then you know what I mean. How about food that's branded as wholesome, but turns out to be extremely high in sugar or sodium, or automobiles that claim safety as their first priority but in reality possess potentially fatal flaws?

> When a brand's reality fails to live up its promise, we have a brand identity crisis.

Since brand lives in the minds of customers, they are the ones who ultimately control the brand perception based on their actual experiences, no matter what you might say in your ads or tout on your website. And if you're suffering from a brand identity crisis, they will form a different impression than the one you *want* them to have about you. In these days of social media, people can now expose brand identity crises to millions of people with the click of a mouse. Even the smallest misalignment can undo what months and years of brand marketing have promised.

> The only way to have direct influence on your brand perception and avoid an identity crisis is to make a clear promise and then be certain everything you deliver and communicate is aligned with that promise.

The rest depends on how customers perceive your intentions. If you've intentionally built a Brand Strategy that speaks directly to what those customers need and care about (rather than what *you* need or care about) and you're set up to deliver, then you should be okay.

Branding Myths Shattered

If you're part of a small business, non-profit, or start-up firm with limited resources, you may think branding is beyond your grasp. Not true! Let's dispel that myth and a few others right now.

Myth #1: Branding is difficult and time-consuming

Branding isn't rocket science, but it does require focused thought about what your business should stand for and who you want to reach. Then, you commit to consistently send that message through everything you do. This actually saves time and effort, because you won't need to reinvent yourself with each new activity or program. Sure, spending time up front on the ten Brand Strategy questions in Part 2 may take a few weeks, but it is well worth the effort.

I advise you to get your Brand Strategy in place early, so you can put it into action. No lengthy six month projects or heavy binders of recommendations for me. True, this process is never "done," because you never stop being a steward for your brand once all the processes, websites, and designs are in place. But instead of starting from scratch with each new program, you simply keep an eye on things and regularly do a "system check" on your materials, business practices, customer service, and messaging to ensure your brand is clear and consistent.

Branding should not be a complex process that requires a PhD. This is a simple strategy that helps you define and live your organization's values – and also provides an easy to follow roadmap so employees and partners can verbalize and live those values, too. Living your values, if they're authentic to your organization's core mission, should not be hard. You know what they are; now you need to intentionally decide how to communicate them through everything you do and say.

> Effective branding means avoiding hypocrisy and being consistent with your employees, customers, and partners.

A well thought-out Brand Strategy makes things easier for you by getting everyone on the same page.

Myth #2: Branding is expensive

Effective branding can be achieved on any budget.

I've worked with twelve million dollar budgets and one thousand dollar budgets and no company ever thinks they have enough money, regardless of their size. The real key to effective branding is identifying a clear picture of your ideal customers and developing a benefit or value-driven message that speaks directly to their needs. Once you align customers and benefits, you can work with a designer to create your logo and a writer who'll craft your website copy.

Branding only becomes expensive when you *don't* take time to build a strong Brand Strategy first, because then you're grasping at straws and throwing money away on activities that don't move you forward.

> Brand is not about big budgets; it's about making a promise your target audience cares about, then delivering on it clearly and consistently across all customer touch points.

That is what makes branding effective, not how much you spend. There are thousands of customer touch points and interactions during which you can communicate your brand promise for free, or with little added investment if you get creative. And today with social media and other free or cheap tools, the only cost is time. If you're guided by a strong Brand Strategy, you will ultimately spend less money by doing the right things, rather than wasting money on the wrong things.

Myth #3: Branding is all fluff

Brand equity can make or break a company. If you think branding has no financial impact, consider why private equity firms purchase brands for billions of dollars just to gain control of the brand cache or loyal customer base. Studies tell us a strong brand image leads to increased sales, greater gross margin, and improved ROI (return on investment).[2]

Brand is the reason people pay three times as much for a white T-shirt at Nordstrom than they would at Target. It's the reason people ask for Coke at a restaurant, then order water if the place only serves Pepsi. And it's the reason the exact same couch may look hip and sleek at Pottery Barn, but appear boring and plain at a discount store.

> An effective brand directly translates into bottom-line sales.

If you build a brand and communicate it to the right people at the right time, you'll attract the interested customers you seek. In addition, a strong brand guides other marketing decisions that fuel your company's growth, including where to advertise, who to partner with, and how to price your product. Those decisions are anything but fluff: they are the lifeblood of your organization.

---

[2] National Textile Center: Annual Report, *"The Pivotal Role of Brand Image in Purchase Decisions,"* (October 2009)

Myth #4: All designers are the same

All designers and branding firms are not the same. While you can save a lot of money by thinking through a Brand Strategy on your own, you'll need a good designer to bring the visual aspects to life and make your brand appealing. Some designers get it, while others don't. When I worked for a corporation and hired outside vendors, I always turned to the right designer for advice instead of relying on someone's nephew, a high school art student, or an in-house computer programmer.

If a prospective designer doesn't ask about your target audience and what you'd like to convey to your customers and clients, then you should run the other way. A designer who only charges $100 can cost you a lot of money in sales by not communicating the right message. Likewise, don't ask one of your software developers to create a logo or website simply because he knows Adobe Illustrator or HTML programming. Just as someone who knows how to put pen to paper may not be a good writer, programmers are not graphic designers or branding consultants.

Graphic design is a skill.

> Good designers understand how imagery, font, color, shape, and spacing impact the subconscious connections people make about your company.

They know how to take a verbal message and communicate it visually. And they should be experienced enough to give you clear recommendations and push back if you are going in the wrong direction.

You'll be pleased with the results if you craft a strong Brand Strategy on your own first as your guide and then spend a bit more money to work with a designer who'll get it right from the start.

Myth #5: Branding works immediately

Branding and direct response marketing are two different things. Before a brand sticks, people need to experience it over time and in different ways. After all, brand is visual, verbal, *and* experiential, as we discussed. Nike's swoosh didn't have meaning within the first three months it appeared. No one knew what Ben and Jerry were about until news of their socially responsible brand and practices started to spread. And before Disney was *Disney*, with all the imagination, magic, and family entertainment it represents, the company was just an animator named Walt Disney who had big dreams.

Starbucks began as a little-known coffee company in 1971, but in 1982 Howard Schulz began transforming the brand into the coffee powerhouse we know today. Schulz made brand changes and then held fast to his vision of what Starbucks could mean to customers, community, and society in general. He never wavered as he carefully built the company's marketing and brand around that vision.

Branding and messaging evolve over time as customers respond to them. You may be tired of your brand and messaging after three months, but that doesn't mean all your potential customers have had a chance to see it and form an opinion. A marketing research guideline suggests people need to see a marketing message five to seven times before they act on it.

While you may live, eat, and breathe your brand on a daily basis, others need a chance to see it more than once and respond.

If the message is different every time they see it, then you're always starting from zero with your target audience. Give the brand messages and visuals time to work their magic before deciding to pull the plug. As long as your direction is focused and you're consistent across media, you should give the brand concept six months to one year to heat up before you decide if it's working.

Avoid the temptation to change things every few months in an effort to boost quarterly sales growth. If you spend time up front making the best decisions about your Brand Strategy *before* you implement it, then you won't feel the need for major changes later.

Think long and hard before you flip the switch on a logo or brand positioning.

If you get consistent feedback that things aren't working, then you know it's time to make a change. When Pepsi altered their Tropicana juice carton packages in 2009, the new cartons were bland and generic looking. Responding to intense public outcry, Pepsi's CMO, David Burwick conceded: "Sometimes you land in a great place, and sometimes you don't. And when you don't, you need to find a better place. Fast."[3]

Branding vs. PR vs. Marketing vs. Social Media ... Oh My!

Along with believing brand is the same thing as a logo, people often confuse branding with public relations and marketing plans. In reality, brand is the foundation of all other aspects of your marketing plan: it shouldn't come after the fact.

[3] Linda Tischler, *"Never Mind! Pepsi Pulls Much-loathed Tropicana Packaging,"* http://wwwFastCompany.com (February 23, 2009)

Press releases, advertising, social media, and even price promotions are marketing tactics that should be grounded in Brand Strategy. Doing so makes it easier to make decisions such as where to advertise, whether to buy a booth at a particular event, and where to send press releases.

With that in mind, let's put definitions around these terms to keep things straight. Think of this as Marketing 101.

Branding and Marketing Are Not the Same

Marketing is the umbrella term for bringing a product to market and ultimately getting customers to purchase. If any of you suffered through business school as I did, you learned about the **Four P's of Marketing: product, price, place, and promotion:**

1. Product (or Service) – What do we sell and how do we make it?
2. Price – How much do we charge for it?
3. Place – Where and how do we get it to our end consumers?
4. Promotion – How do we get people to know it exists and convince them to buy it?

So, broadly, marketing is about bringing products or services to "market" and effectively selling them. Too often, small business owners only think of marketing in terms of the fourth P, Promotion. But marketing encompasses so much more. Sub-functions that fall under the marketing umbrella include:

- Advertising
- Communications
- Database marketing
- Direct marketing

- Event organization
- Field marketing
- Global marketing
- International marketing
- Internet marketing
- Industrial marketing
- Market research
- Public relations
- Product marketing
- Media relations/Press
- Retailing
- Lead generation campaigns
- Search engine marketing
- Social influence marketing
- Social media
- Pricing
- Market research
- Competitive analysis

Many companies roll all the strategies and tactics within these subcategories into a collective marketing plan. The corporate marketing plan is a strategic overview of tactics and themes each group will execute during the year: What ads will be placed, where will those ads go, and what will be the main messages? On which markets will we focus? What products will we promote at different times of the year? What is the product release schedule? What is the competition doing this year? What customer acquisition campaigns or events will take place?

Brand forms the foundation of your overall marketing strategy, but is not the *same thing* as a marketing strategy. Brand touches much more than marketing and can serve as a litmus test for your operations, hiring practices, distribution strategy, and partner criteria.

People often believe advertising and branding are interchangeable and mean the same thing. They don't. Advertising is a marketing tactic based on the Brand Strategy. Advertising is one more vehicle to communicate your brand message and promise to the world. Brand positioning should be thought out before you create an advertisement.

The beauty of owning a small business is that things are far less complicated and you have a huge opportunity to get this right where the big guys might trip up. If you're new and just launching a business, this is the perfect time to build your Brand Strategy. Decide on the brand *before* you advertise, so you won't spend precious time and money chasing your tail.

As a small business owner, you don't need a complicated marketing plan. A Brand Strategy can show you what you need and don't need. Being small means you're close to your customers and all decisions stem from you. This means you call the shots and make sure all the pieces align. Being nimble and having a small employee count can help you embrace that strength and build your brand right from the start.

Branding Is Not Public Relations

To keep it simple, think of public relations (PR) as media, awards, and speaking engagements. Public relations means communicating information to various audiences, downplaying negative information, and elevating positive information in order to improve your company's reputation and give credibility to your products or services. As one implement in the toolbox of promotion, PR lives under the broad umbrella of marketing and should be included in most marketing plans.

But PR targets different audiences and
metrics and intended outcomes than other n
you may use. Since PR is about getting th'
about you, it tends to be viewed as more credible
advertising. For example, a targeted PR campaign mig-
establish your company or executives as trusted experts
in your field. Radio interviews, local TV appearances,
speaking to local groups, and writing articles for community
newspapers fit this category.

The goal of PR is to gain awareness, establish credibility,
and get your name out there – perhaps by educating your
target audience about your products and services in a softer
way than pure advertising. But keep in mind that PR won't
necessarily create new customers for your products because
it isn't a direct marketing channel. If you expect this, you'll
be disappointed.

Many small business owners think PR is synonymous with
"marketing plan" or branding. I've heard too many small
business owners say: "My marketing/Brand Strategy this
year is to do four press releases each month." A marketing
plan should be much more than public relations and press
releases. As I hope I've shown, PR is only one tactic within
your larger marketing plan.

The Brand Strategy shapes your PR messages and target
media lists. If brand is the story you tell, then PR is about
making sure that story is heard. It helps you increase
exposure by linking your product or service to timely stories
in the news. What PR cannot do is create a brand where
none exists, or worse, make people think your brand is
something it's not. That might work for a little while, but
your customers will soon catch on.

I read that Karen Hughes, former communications advisor to George W. Bush, had taken a job at high profile PR firm Burston Marstellar in 2008.[4]

Oddly enough, Karen was going to work with former Hillary Clinton campaign manager, Mark Penn. They billed themselves as a "bipartisan brain trust" on strategy and crisis communication.

I found it amusing to read that Hughes "left her State Department position ... after making little progress on her mission to improve the U.S. image around the world." This was in 2008, when the United States' "brand" was taking a global beating. Wow. Talk about an uphill battle. No wonder PR gets a bad rap – people expect it to perform miracles.

Here's the thing: PR can't just come along and make you thinner, prettier, or more popular if the fundamentals aren't in place – if the *brand promise* isn't met. Many CEOs think they can operate poorly, slap a coat of public relations over everything, and their reputation will be magically transformed. Life doesn't work that way. Public relations can bring good things to light and even downplay bad things, but it won't conjure up news or goodwill from thin air. You'd be better off hiring a magician.

Back to Karen Hughes: *The Wall Street Journal* article went on to say "despite traveling around the globe – sometimes accompanied by U.S. sports stars – and beefing up the public-diplomacy budget, Ms. Hughes wasn't able to change the world's view of the U.S., according to polls showing the Iraq War continued to harm America's image."

I'm not making any political statements here, but all companies can learn a lesson from this. People aren't as

---

[4] Monica Langley, *The Wall Street Journal,* "Clinton, Bush Advisors Steeped in Crisis Join Forces," (July 9, 2008)

stupid as we'd like to believe, and it's best not to try and force feed a message to them. You can say something over and over, but if you haven't delivered on that clear brand promise – if poor product choices, bad environmental practices, or rude customer service have been the status quo – then no amount of well-placed media articles and glossy, shallow, movie star parades will change that.

In the end, it all comes down to your organization's DNA and what your customers – and employees – see and experience.

Are you consistently *living* your brand promise?

Companies that think good PR will erase broken promises are kidding themselves. If it were that easy, everyone would be doing it. If your brand experience isn't clear and consistent, no amount of PR can make people think it is, just because you say so.

Branding Is Not Social Media

(ring, ring)
Me: "Red Slice, Maria speaking."

Client: "Hi Maria, my name is Sue and I own a small business here in town. I've heard you're one of the best branding experts on the planet *(note: artistic license taken during this reenactment)*. I'm looking for branding help."

Me: "Excellent! Why don't you tell me a bit about your goals and what you are looking to achieve?"

Client: "Well, I hear social media is all the rage and I need to get in on that. Can I hire you to build my Facebook fan page?"

Me: "We have great Facebook partners if that's what you need, but it's best to work on your Brand Strategy first and talk about your benefits, differentiators, and your target audience. Then we can decide if you even need a Fan Page. Having the Brand Strategy helps you spend your limited marketing dollars and time wisely."

Client: "But, that's what I'm saying. I know my Brand Strategy. It's to build a Facebook fan page."

Me: "Okay, so tell me a bit about what your brand is all about. What's your mission and who is your ideal customer?"

Client: "I sell those modified cell phones. You know, the ones with the big numbers and really simple functions for elderly people who can't see very well. Many of those folks are tech-averse and don't need all the bells and whistles on their phone. So when can we start on a Facebook fan page? Oh, and can you help with Twitter, too?"

Me: "Well, Facebook and Twitter are just tactics – part of an overall marketing plan. And the marketing plan is based on a strong Brand Strategy. Putting all of that aside, may I ask if the folks buying these phones are on Facebook and Twitter? With their sight issues and dislike of technology, are they even on the Internet?"

Client: "Well, isn't everyone on Facebook and Twitter these days?"

Me: "Many people are, but if you're working with a limited budget, I'm not sure Facebook and Twitter are the best ways to reach the specific people who need your product. It would help to sit down and walk through your Brand Strategy, which includes looking at your ideal buying audience. Then, we can hone in on the best choices for your time and money."

Client: "Well, I'm not sure I have the time or money for all that. I just want to get the Facebook fan page and

Twitter thing going, because I keep hearing that's how to get customers."

You can see where this is going.

Social media is not hype or a fad. These real-time applications have changed business relationships by creating an instant two-way conversation between company and customer that leads to more loyalty, and ultimately, more purchases.

Starbucks has great success with social media and uses it to launch new products and promotions via its rabid online evangelists. Many of their ideal customers are all over social media and are often tech-savvy. I recently heard Starbucks' "official Twitterer" speak at a luncheon. He said social media is an effective way for them to monitor feedback on new products, make corporate changes, conduct launches, and even adapt customer service. Beats the old Suggestion Box any day of the week.

Companies that are open and agile can leverage social media and react in a heartbeat to suggestions and crises.

But until something comes along to change my mind, I will stand behind this mantra:

> Social media is not a brand strategy. It is *part* of your brand strategy.

You can think of social media as just one tactic, one vehicle (albeit a unique, interactive, viral one) through which you communicate your brand to the world. As I like to tell clients and audiences: "Starting a Twitter account is not a marketing plan or a Brand Strategy."

Social media isn't right for every company. I know dozens of great social media strategists who give sound advice, do great work, and know how to leverage Twitter, Facebook, and the rest. I often recommend my clients work with them – but only if the client's Brand Strategy points to social media as an effective vehicle.

Even social media experts agree that you should have a fully-baked Brand Strategy *before* you dive into execution. You have to know what story you're telling and to whom before putting it out there.

I might be a lone voice in the wind on this one, but I don't believe every company needs a Twitter account, a Facebook fan page, or even a blog. **It all depends on your target audience and your brand promise.** You need to communicate your brand and your message through vehicles that will reach your target audience and be effective. If they use social media to make buying decisions and interact with brands like yours, then absolutely, you should extend your brand to those channels.

In addition, if your Brand Strategy isn't well thought-out, then how do you know what to communicate in these social media vehicles? Social media should extend the messaging expressed through your other marketing activities; it doesn't live in isolation. Brand is the content. Social media is the channel to communicate that brand out to the world and let customers interact with you.

Here's another big issue with social media: it can be unforgiving if you create an inauthentic relationship – a loosey-goosey brand promise with no substance behind it. Scott Montgomery sees many companies using social media the wrong way, with transparent "seeded" comments and overly-pushy promotional messages that are all one-sided. Talk about getting kicked off the island. Not only is Scott grounded in brand fundamentals, he's also co-founder of Fizziolo.gy (www.fiziolo.gy), a company that tracks, analyzes, and mines social media chatter. He sees the biggest branding successes in social media from **enthusiast brands...**

"...those that can offer value through social engagement, and those that are creating a bit of controversy. Google, for example, wins in social media not just because they engage in it, but by the fact that their innovations are worth tweeting about. I can't tell you how often we've seen Google Wave as a trending topic on Twitter, not because of active seeding, but because their tactics have got people talking – releasing controversial videos of Wave in action, beta-testing by invitation – that sort of thing. I'm certainly not ruling out some kinds of seeding, but it's all the more powerful if you devise your product's strategy to be inherently "political." By that I mean, create things where the audience has a reason to take your side (or at least *a* side). Let your product efforts, promotions and events be retweetable."[5]

If this book does anything for you, I hope it convinces you that branding and marketing aren't the same, that promotion and PR are not the only aspects of marketing, and that social media *extends* a strong brand, but it is not a Brand Strategy in and of itself. Now that we're all speaking the same language, we'll explore why Brand Strategy matters to your business and why it isn't all fluff and hype.

Why Does Brand Matter?

What can brand do for you? Just as we respect and admire people who know who they are and what they want, brand helps organizations attract the right customers and make sales more easily.

---

[5] Maria Ross, *Red Slice: Ask the Expert: Using social media to delight*

> Brand *clarity* attracts customers and brand *consistency* makes them stick around.

As customers encounter your brand in various situations they'll remember you, slot you into the right part of their brains, and your brand will stick. The more you fulfill the brand promise in everything you do, the more you'll solidify your brand to the people who matter most. Your Brand Strategy is the tool that helps you accomplish this. For every operational decision (hiring, pricing, advertising, customer service, marketing, design, copy, etc.), you should ask yourself, "Does this accurately reflect my brand to the customers I want?" If the answer is no, then make changes!

In addition, a strong Brand Strategy enables you to do more with less.

> Rather than wasting money and time on the wrong activities, a Brand Strategy helps you laser-focus on activities and messages that will have the greatest impact.

With the tight budgets and time constraints common to small businesses, start-up firms, and non-profits, this is a necessity. Brand Strategy isn't about quantity – it's about quality. Even if you can only afford limited marketing activities, a strong Brand Strategy will help you make sure each of them packs a powerful punch.

What's Your Reason for Being?

When it comes right down to it, we're in business to make money. But unless you know the true essence of what your business is all about and its impact on people's lives, you'll be stuck on the lowest rung of the ladder. In a competitive market where many new businesses fail, that's a death sentence.

Marty Neumeier, Director of Transformation at Liquid Agency (www.liquidagency) and author of **The Brand Gap** and **Zag** suggests giving yourself the Obituary Test to figure out your reason for being: Write the obituary of your business in 25 years and outline what you did that was great and why the world is a better place because your company existed.

"When you do this, you see something bigger. You see how every symbol, message, and action you put out into the world creates a brand legacy in the minds of customers, which is really where brand lives in the first place," Marty says. He advises this will not only attract the right employees to grow your business, but will impact everything you do. "When you open a business just to make money, you can lose heart."

A clear Brand Strategy, based on your larger reason for being, makes it easier to focus your organization's activities around one true cause. It helps you easily determine what products or services to offer, how to price them, what your logo should convey, what experience your website should evoke, and even what colors to use. Making such decisions without a strong brand foundation is akin to throwing darts at a moving target. You'll waste time and money with designers, website programmers, and writers because either everything will look good, or nothing will. Without a guidepost, any road looks like the right one, even if it leads to a dead end!

Building a Brand That Can Change with the Times

A tried-and-true business strategy is to ask yourself what business you are actually in. There is an old adage that asks: "Am I in the horse and buggy business or the transportation business?" In the early 1900s, many companies in the *horse and buggy business* went under when automobiles came out. But if you were in *the transportation business,* you could have changed the buggies into automobiles or branched into something else transportation-related. If you clung to the horse and buggy business, then you didn't understand your customers' true needs. People didn't need buggies per se – they needed a way to Grandma's house on Christmas Eve. The lesson: don't put yourself in a box, leaving no room to adapt and grow.

This kind of thinking allows you to understand and meet your customers' needs. As Red Slice, I help organizations tell their stories. My mission is to engage, inform, and delight audiences. This approach inspires my clients and helps me do a better job for them. It also separates me from my competition, who just offers marketing services.

If your brand can address a fundamental or inspirational need, then you can see things through your customer's eyes and this kind of positioning will inspire customer loyalty beyond your imagination.

Ever see the movie *Jerry Maguire?* In one scene, Dorothy (Renee Zellweger) agrees to leave the security of a bigger agency and follow Jerry (Tom Cruise) to his new, independent sports agency venture – all because of Jerry's mission statement. The new mission statement defined the true role of sports agents: to stop being driven by money and spend more time helping clients achieve their dreams.

When Dorothy explains why she took a chance and went to work with him, she says, "Mostly, I just want to be inspired."

Inspiration is something we all crave. Human beings want to know, consciously or subconsciously, that their efforts are going toward a higher purpose. Even a small dose of inspiration can ignite a sense of purpose and get people to do amazing things for the good of the company and its customers.

A Brand Strategy can lead to this inspiration, because it helps give your business a mission and a vision. I've worked for start-up firms that considered Brand Strategy a "fluffy" component and only cared about going public. Not only did these workplaces lack soul and heart, they also had no rudder to help us determine the most effective marketing strategies. So we focused on a feature war with competitors ("We have this new widget." "Oh, yeah? Well, we have that widget, plus two more!") As employees, we had no idea why we were putting in thankless 12-hour days. If you can't delight and inspire your employees, you won't be able to delight and inspire customers.

These examples will help you focus on the "higher calling" of your business:

Are you a graphic designer, OR do you solve your clients' communication challenges?

Do you sell baby clothes, OR do you help mothers economize and pass on a sense of style to their children?

Do you make computers and technology, OR do you challenge the status quo (hello, Apple)?

Are you a jewelry designer, OR do you create memories?

Don't become so esoteric that no one can tell what you actually do, but you do need to separate yourself from the pack and go in at a deeper level to withstand market changes and commoditization. In other words: go beyond "increase profits" and "reduce costs," the generic marketing message.

Check out this boilerplate message from one of Apple's press releases:[6]

> 66Apple ignited the personal computer revolution in the 1970s with the Apple II and reinvented the personal computer in the 1980s with the Macintosh. Today, Apple continues to lead the industry in innovation with its award-winning computers, OS X operating system, and iLife and professional applications. Apple is also spearheading the digital media revolution with its iPod portable music and video players and iTunes online store, and has entered the mobile phone market with its revolutionary iPhone.99

According to this, Apple ignites revolutions, reinvents, leads the industry in innovation, and spearheads the digital media revolution. Definitely more inspiring than "manufactures computers and other digital equipment," isn't it? Do Apple's competitors occupy the same space in people's brains and are they in the same "business?" Tom Asacker, a prominent brand speaker and author (www.acleareye.com) verbalizes the idea of purpose and motivation when he writes:

> 66People are not inspired by your pursuits or your status. They're inspired – and come to life – by their pursuits. They want their work and their lives to be stimulating, meaningful, and to make a difference to others. Nietzsch wrote, 'He who has a why to live can bear with almost any how.' Without a why – a why to reach and stretch, a why to proffer ideas, a why to treat customers and coworkers with love and respect, a why to go the extra mile, a why to be committed to excellence, a why to go to work in the morning – all the hows, whats, whens, and what fors, become empty rhetoric.99

[6] www.apple.com

Rabid Fans: Your Logo Should Be My Tattoo

Companies that completely understand their brand are the ones wno connect with customers and inspire loyalty.

I heard a great story from consultant Simon Sinek[7] at an entrepreneur's conference in 2008.

Midway through his presentation, he polled the audience of women business owners:

"How many of you have your company logo tattooed on your body?"

Amused, we looked around to see if anyone raised a hand.

"Seriously, how many of you have your company logo tattooed on your body?

Nervous laughter rose from the crowd. A bead of sweat broke out on my forehead. Should I be saying yes? But that was preposterous!

As Simon continued, he asked us to think about bikers who sport a Harley Davidson tattoo. Oh, now it made sense! Yes, I've seen the tattoo on many a passing motorcyclist in the Northern California hills. And then I connected the dots. That Harley tattoo is just another company logo. Customers feel such fierce loyalty to the brand and products that they ink themselves permanently, like walking billboards. The brand *means* something to them and says something about their identity. They're part of the Harley "tribe." They identify with it so much that they permanently marked their bodies with a corporate logo. Talk about rabid fans. Those tattoo-inked customers are the best salespeople the company could ask for – and Harley doesn't pay them a dime. What business wouldn't want customers who pay out of their own pockets

---

[7] http://sinekpartners.com

to become walking billboards, and not only that, they loyally purchase more and more products? You think the guy or gal with a permanent Harley tattoo will be swayed by Honda's or Suzuki's advertising? Heck no.

When was the last time you felt so strongly about a product that you tattooed the logo on your arm? The very thought of people running around with Taco Bell or Walmart tattoos makes me giggle. But Harley riders feel a connection, a kinship, with the brand that only vaguely has to do with motorcycles. It means so much more. Harley is about freedom, rebellion, the open road, adventure, strength, and camaraderie.

That's the power of a strong brand promise. The promise is more than a product; it's a statement, a reputation, and lifestyle that resonates with customers.

When you create a "tribe" for your product or service, word of mouth marketing becomes a snap, because tribe members influence one another.

Don't Leave it to Chance: People Will Form Their Own Brand Impressions

Every company has a brand, whether they know it or not. As stated earlier, brand is the "mind share" you take up in someone's brain – the parts that light up when they hear your name, see your logo, or buy your product. And guess what? Even if you believe this is a bunch of marketing mumbo jumbo, let me be clear: People will form an opinion about your business no matter what you do or don't do. No matter what action you take, they'll assign you a brand and form an opinion. Doesn't it make prudent business sense to get in front of that and influence the brand, so you can be sure it fits your business goals?

I once worked for a dot com during the Internet boom of the late 90s and early '00s. We were a competitor to E-Loan and Lending Tree and offered online loans and credit cards. This dot com didn't survive the bust for several reasons, but that's for another book. One thing we did well was build a strong brand. This was exciting to do from scratch, the right way, from day one – before we crafted any ads, logos, or messaging.

Back in those early Internet days, people didn't trust their financial data to online sites so we needed to build a brand of trust and warmth to get people to share their precious financial information. After a strong Brand Strategy and research effort – before any advertising was conceived or produced – we created four distinct audience profiles and strategic positioning to represent where we fit against our competition. Visually, we chose yellow as our primary color to stand out from other traditional institutions that tended to use green or blue. Research told us yellow was the color most closely associated with customer advocacy. We used illustrations on the site rather than photos, and we adopted a casual tone in our copy to lend a safe, warm, whimsical air.

We competed not only with other online lending sites, but also with the traditional image of big bad banks – overweight, balding, white, male fat cats behind mahogany desks. These hallowed institutions screamed stiff, formal, and foreboding and only let people into "the club" who looked and sounded just like them. We wanted to be the welcoming brand of "Yes" where even the disenfranchised customers rejected by traditional banks would be treated fairly and find a loan or credit card just for them. We wanted good, honest, hardworking people who were intimidated by "the club" to find a place that cared about them and their dreams and would help them achieve success.

We endured heated arguments with certain technical engineers and programmers who thought the resulting brand was fluffy, cartoonish, and unnecessary. They fought us at every turn as we tried to inject this brand into the website design, the advertising strategy, and the PR outreach. Internally, we even trained our call center staff on the brand to ensure they adopted the right tone on the telephone with customers. I'll never forget the words of one senior technical executive who sniffed, "Look at Google. Look at Craig's List. They're simple black and white interfaces that get results. We look like clowns. People just want credible information and to get data, period. They don't need bells and whistles."

But he failed to see that being "functional" and "utilitarian" is still a brand choice. Google and Craig's List worked well in simple formats because it fit their brand promise at the time. Google's clean interface of a search box and a small graphic communicated "No muss, no fuss" in finding exactly what you were looking for within the vast Internet labyrinth. That was their brand promise and the interface delivered it. Craig's List was trying to move people from newspaper classifieds to the web in a big way. They needed basic categories like a newspaper, since all posts were user-generated ads. They wanted to be the "no-frills, grassroots, power-to-the-people, community-based-technology-for-the-rest-of-us" brand.

Google and Craig's List didn't ask people to invest a high level of personal, confidential data. We, on the other hand, tried to convince customers who didn't trust traditional banks in the first place to not only perform financial functions online, but to feel comfortable sharing sensitive financial data with us. And in 1999, this was something most people just didn't do. So, we needed to create a brand that was a) different from the industry that had rejected them in the past and b) approachable, warm, and inviting.

I can proudly say that this strategy would have been extremely effective – had the company not gone under due to other causes. Based on this strong Brand Strategy, the advertising increased our loan application rates by over 100% in our 14 target markets, just two weeks into the multi-channel ad campaign based on radio spots alone; the TV, print, and billboard components hadn't even hit those markets yet. I've chuckled over the years as traditional banks have adopted an almost identical Brand Strategy, some even using our "yes" verbiage.

Here's another example: My husband and I want to love and support a special local bookstore in our neighborhood. Based on location, name, and visual identity, the store promises a warm, personal book buying experience unlike the big box book stores. Unfortunately, my husband was turned off by an incident that didn't seem important at the time. One day when we entered the store, someone behind us left the door open as we walked in and they walked out. The clerk glanced up, saw the open door, and headed over in a huff to close it. Her body language told us she was miffed and assumed we were to blame. She nearly pushed us out of the way in her haste to make a point and shut the door. How was that attitude personal and warm?

I'm sure the storeowner didn't *mean* for this to be our experience, but that owner failed to ensure his employees were warm and friendly. Because one clerk didn't live up to the store's brand, we now have a negative perception of the place as snooty and cold. At first my husband couldn't figure out why shopping there made him uncomfortable, but then recalled this seemingly insignificant incident.

The lesson to small business owners is this:

> Since brand is experience, perception, and "mind share," you're going to have a brand whether you mean to or not. And every little choice you make or don't make will affect that brand.

People will file your business away in certain parts of their brain, as humans tend to do when processing information. They're going to assume who you serve and decide if you're right for them. Are you for tweens or old ladies? Do you represent high-end lasting quality or trendy and cheap?

As customers interact with your business in hundreds of different ways, they will form opinions and tell their friends. Wouldn't you rather influence their perception with consistent messaging and experience, rather than leave it up to fate? I know I would.

How to Avoid Random Acts of Marketing: Brand Strategy as Your Foundation

Without a Brand Strategy, how the heck can you decide
- what to offer and to whom,
- how to price it,
- what colors or graphics to use in your logo, based on what you want to communicate,
- what tone your copy needs to take,
- what publications to advertise in,
- what type of employees to hire,
- what partners to play with?

If you don't have a grounded Brand Strategy, you're all over the place, grasping at whatever new trend or opportunity is in front of you on any given day. I call this "performing random acts of marketing." And if you're confused, don't you think customers will feel the same? Let me ask it this way: Would you put up drywall and build a façade for a house with no foundation poured or studs in place? You have to do one thing before the other or the whole structure will collapse. Same principle with brand.

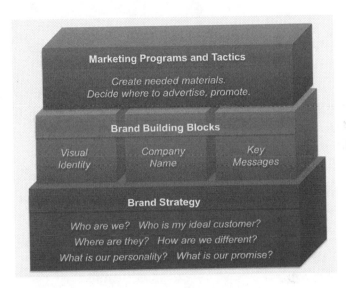

The previous figure illustrates a good way to look at Brand Strategy and what it can do for you. You'll see that building the Brand Strategy first creates a firm foundation. We'll explore that foundation through the key Brand Strategy questions in Part 2 of this book.

The Brand Strategy questions are designed to help you think about who you serve, what you represent, why you're different, and what value you offer. They also help you focus on your ideal customer. If you don't know who and where your buyers are, you'll spend time and money on the wrong things and end up poking your eye out with a sharp stick in frustration because nothing will work.

Brand as Investment Guidepost

You have a great business idea. So you immediately contact a marketing consultant or designer and request the following:

- Logo
- Website
- Brochures
- Business cards
- Letterhead

Hold on a sec. Yes, those are basic marketing communications vehicles, but without factoring in your ideal audience and the way they need to interact with you and your brand, how do you know if you need all these elements? For example, I communicate with my clients mostly over email. Do I need to print thousands of sheets of linen letterhead that will only be scanned, faxed, and never appreciated? Will customers find you through referrals from friends who've already seen and experienced your product? If that's the case, do you need a 15-page brochure when a one-page fact sheet will fill in the blanks for them?

Know how your customers need to find and interact with you before you create everything under the sun and end up a year from now dumping all those lovely brochures into the recycle bin.

When attending trade shows, business people assume they need printed materials on hand at the booth. Upon signing up for an event, their gut reaction is to say "What brochures will we need?" Whoa, fella. Let's take a step back. Who are the people at this show? What other sponsors will be there? How will attendees consume information? Are they flying here and already loaded down with luggage? If so, your expensive 4-color brochures will end up in the hotel trashcan, and then where will we be? Are they coming specifically to see you, or will you have competition around? Maybe you only need to give people an item that will help them remember your name so they can get more detailed information on your website.

Know thy audience and thy brand and you will know the best communication and marketing tactics in which to invest. Translation: only pay for things that will get you more buzz among the right target audience and will ultimately lead to sales.

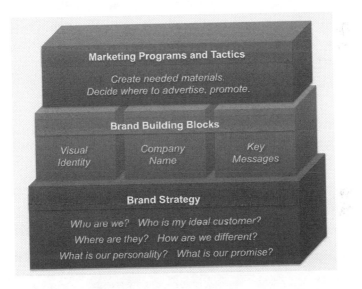

As the figure above shows, once you've answered the key questions and created your overall Brand Strategy, you can use the answers and data you've collected for what I call the Brand Building Blocks. These are basic items every company needs to mix and match in order to do the rest of their marketing. The building blocks include your company name if you don't already have one (or may inspire you to change your name), your visual identity (logo, colors, imagery), and key messages. Based on your benefits and audience, for example, you can select a meaningful name that's memorable, easy to spell and pronounce, stands out from your competition, and communicates something about your values, benefits, and differentiating factors to your target audience. Or you can choose company colors that resonate with your target audience, communicate the proper emotions and "feel" of your brand, or help you stand out among competitors.

If you haven't thought about your target audience in detail, you may miss choosing a name that will attract them and communicate your brand promise all by itself. Of course you'll need to check if the name is available for trademark and if the right website URL is available, but this exercise will help you select a name that has impact. Once you have the right name for your business, you'll be able to select a logo and know what key messages to craft, based on the information in your Brand Strategy. We will talk more about applying brand to these items in Part 3 of this book.

Celebriducks, a quirky little company, became extremely successful because they articulated a unique brand promise before they even started the company. They use that strategy to guide all of their decisions, as you'll see from the Brand At Work case study that follows.

BRAND AT WORK: CELEBRIDUCKS

A differentiated brand must be clear and fire on all cylinders in order to stand out from the crowd. This is especially true if you have a quirky, unique brand that some people may not "get." CelebriDucks (www.CelebriDucks. com) went all-out in creating their brand before launching the company. CelebriDucks is the original creator of the first-ever celebrity rubber ducks representing the greatest icons of film, music, athletics, and history. Are you familiar with baseball player bobbleheads? They're kind of like that. CelebriDucks have been produced for the NBA, MLB, NHL, NASCAR, NCAA collegiate mascots, and numerous Fortune 500 companies. They were voted one of the top 100 gifts by *Entertainment Weekly* and their line includes everyone from Elvis Presley and Marilyn Monroe to the world's first ever 100 percent recycled "Green" duck. The company has pioneered a whole new collectible with over 200 different CelebriDucks to date.

CelebriDucks' brand is meant to be cool, whimsical, and "outside-the-box." They appeal to someone looking for a unique, fun, and well-crafted gift. Each duck is intricately sculpted and painted and arrives in a gorgeous gift box. "We knew from the start that our brand is an attitude and our corporate point of view, reflected in the products we create," says Craig Wolfe, President. "We set out to craft the most classy, unique, and innovative rubber ducks on the market.

Cool and classy ... rubber ducks? Most definitely. Celebri-Ducks is a higher-end brand, offering something different: they know their target customers will pay well for that one-of-a-kind experience. "When people want boring and cheap, we send them to another company," says Craig. "We are more expensive than almost every rubber duck on the market and there's a reason for it. We're different!" This brand promise extends to their decisions about distribution and advertising: they avoid being distributed in discount environments and when they advertise, they only choose high quality partners.

Being different and unique permeates everything the company does – even product line choices. "We never wanted to be like everyone else from day one. We knew no one did licensed rubber ducks, no one else used top flight gift boxes for ducks, no one really cared to sculpt and paint with a detail that was unknown in the industry. And half of the ducks on the market did not even float correctly. Then along came CelebriDucks, which changed the landscape." Has such a unique and bold brand paid off? You bet? The company has been featured on CNN and hundreds of other media outlets. CelebriDucks is also the only one licensed to do the mascots for the top universities in the U.S., celebrities, and major film studios. Companies such as P&G and Amazon now come to them to be added to the line. Such success is certainly nothing to quack at.

Brand as Asset

Brand can be a powerful asset for any business, large or small. The strongest brands can even stay alive after death. What comes to mind when you hear massage chairs and ionic air purifiers? Ah, Sharper Image. Many a boring Saturday was spent meandering around those stores and testing gadgets. But alas, the chain went bankrupt.

But wait ... don't count them out. In 2008, two of the country's largest retail liquidators, Hilco and Gordon Brothers, resurrected the brand to live on in the virtual sense. Other retailers who want to bask in the glow of Sharper Image's hard-earned brand equity can license it to make their own gadgets more appealing.

This is the power of brand. The company name creates such a strong mental association, that licensing the name after the company folded is worth money. I bet when the CFO's of those liquidators cash their licensing checks, no one is saying "branding is just fluffy marketing stuff," now are they?

Here's the part I love. The fact that Sharper Image still wanted to maintain an upscale, quality brand association as they closed. They dictated rules around the look of the "Store Closing" signs at retail locations' close-out sales: "No bright orange signs. You can't be too schlocky" they said. Now that's a real understanding of how to maintain brand promise.[8]

While ultimately the name of the game is "sales figures," I tend to think of sales as the market share or "wallet share" you get from customers. And we all know that's the most important measure of success. But brand is the "mind share" you get from customers. You'll be in a much more powerful place for long-term success if you can capture the mind share that leads to the wallet share, rather than propping up short-term results with random gimmicks, discounts, or specials that don't invite ongoing loyalty.

> You want a brand that elevates you above a commodity.

Brand as Competitive Weapon

Inside my mind lives a curmudgeonly business owner (or CEO, or VP of Engineering) named Sam. Sam thinks marketing is a bunch of hooey that lies to people and wastes time and money. Sam believes goods and services are bought and sold based on quality and a conscious need – period. Let's say he sells picture frames and photo album supplies. Sam doesn't market to a particular group, because he feels

---

[8] Jeffrey McCracken and Peter Lattman, *The Wall Street Journal,* "Sharper Image Lives – As a Brand," (June 26, 2008)

anyone who takes pictures at any time might have a need for these items.

"I don't need that branding baloney," he huffs. "People who want picture frames will buy my picture frames when they need them. My products are nice-looking, good quality, and I treat people fairly. I sell the best picture and album supplies out there."

One day another business owner, Heather, also decides to sell picture frames and album supplies. She might even sell the same ones Sam does, from the same manufacturers. But as an avid photographer, Heather has a greater mission with her company: she wants to help people preserve cherished memories and imbue their homes and offices with style and personality. This immediately differentiates her from Sam. She sees picture frames as an extension of home décor, so deciding on the right ones is an important decision.

Heather carefully chooses a warm, fun, and stylish logo and colors to communicate her mission, make her company memorable, and visually appeal to the specific buying audience she has in mind. After all, photo supplies and pictures are all about being aesthetically pleasing – if her logo, colors and entire store decor do not look good, why should anyone trust that her products will look good?

She understands that people may not consciously know why they're drawn to her, but the feelings evoked by her visual elements – her logo, colors, website, signage – have a certain design sensibility customers associate with style and flair. Customers will *want* to buy their picture frames from Heather because of what that says about their own taste and style.

Heather goes beyond the visual to live out her Brand Strategy through the customer buying experience. Her employees are all photographers or people who have a passion for collecting and displaying photos. She even develops a training program and "check out protocol" for her staff to ensure they offer customers advice on the best frames for certain environments or how to display an impressive photo wall. Heather offers classes at her shop for people interesting in scrap booking or photo enhancement, elevating her as a credible photo expert in the mind of her target audience. Lastly, Heather does highly targeted press outreach, only pursuing three to four key publications her target audience reads. She presents herself to the press as the area's best source for photo expertise, even if the article isn't specifically about her shop, but about photography or framing in general.

Heather charges more for her picture frames than Sam. She provides more value with her welcoming shop, her expert advice, and her staff's passion – and she offers a liberal return policy should anyone be dissatisfied.

Sam is perplexed. Why would someone pay twice as much for the same frame, he wonders. We're both selling the same product to someone who has the same need: a picture frame.

But what Sam failed to grasp is that most of us make unconscious buying decisions all the time. He also failed to understand the real unconscious need of his customers, or what is called a *latent* or *dormant* need. This is a need people don't realize they have until they're presented with a better option. Sam's customers probably thought there were only so many ways to frame or display pictures, until Heather presented them with better options and styles. Remember, we all thought cassette tapes were fine until CD's came along, and CD's were fine until we found out you could store MP3's on your computer or iPod and save tons of space in your house.

Heather, on the other hand, not only brought her customers' needs to light by providing stylish options, she also fulfills this need. She speaks to these needs through her messaging, visual elements, and even her company policies and marketing activities. She addresses these needs and the benefits she provides in everything she does. Therefore, she isn't wasting money on every new marketing tactic that comes her way; she knows which will convey her brand messages and reach her target audience in the best way and which will not. So she makes wiser, more targeted use of her slim marketing budget. And she gets results.

Brand doesn't necessarily enable you to charge more for your products or services – sometimes offering the best value at the lowest price is part of the strategy. But brand does tell your story in a way that speaks to customer's subconscious needs and wants – without deceiving them in any way – and they feel a connection. Your messages resonate more deeply with them and they tend to be more loyal as a result. In addition, this connection will cause them to tell others about you and get word of mouth going.

Sam can't merely copy aspects of Heather's business and "slap a coat of brand paint" on his own business. For example, if he tries to offer scrap booking classes without changing anything else, will that fly? Up to this point, everything he's been saying about his business has been commodity-based and utilitarian. Will customers really believe he's the best person to help them artfully preserve their precious memories? Most likely they won't buy it, because they recognize an empty promise. We've all seen companies try to mimic a competitor, usually with disastrous results. A recent example is certain car companies trying to promote environmental responsibility and fuel-efficient models. Our experiences with these brands have shown the companies are trying to take advantage of hot trends without a real corporate commitment to the environment. I'm not saying they can't evolve as a brand or change their ways, but it will take more than slick TV ads before people change their mindset. This will happen over time as our experiences with the brand slowly change and the car company begins to fulfill its promises.

If you've been like Sam and haven't seen the bottom-line, competitive gains a strong brand can provide, there is hope.

> Branding succeeds when it's done *right* and when it's done *authentically* – meaning you don't just talk the talk, but you walk the walk.

Authentic branding can differentiate you from the competition if you stay true to it across everything you do, as it did for Outspoken Media in the Brand at Work case study below.

BRAND AT WORK: OUTSPOKEN MEDIA

With a name like Outspoken Media (www.outspoken media.com), you definitely need to walk your talk. This Troy, NY-based Internet marketing firm does that in spades. The firm was founded by three strong, sassy women who grew tired of corporate-speak from other firms that used fluff and fake promises to gain business. Their brand emphasizes being up-front, honest, transparent, and blunt in doing the right things for clients and getting results. They even have a Chief Branding Officer, Lisa Barone, the voice of the company, who ensures all materials and messages take an honest, outspoken slant, and helps decide on everything from which clients they'll take on to the type of people they hire.

Visually, this shows through on their no-frills, straightforward website. But the brand also plays out in their business decisions, including losing a Fortune 300 client who wanted them to retract a Tweet they posted as a joke. "We had a decision to make in that moment," Lisa says. "Change who we were in order to land the biggest client we've ever had, or stay true to ourselves. We chose the latter and the Tweet still stands."

They refuse to compromise on the truth or their beliefs, and clients can feel good about that. The company even publicly took on a world-renowned marketing guru's brand program they thought was unfairly opt-out versus opt-in, forcing him to change the program due to the press and public outcry. And they've spoken out against other online marketing tactics they feel are not in a business' best interest.

This company surely lives up to its name.

///

We must always remember that, as humans, not all our buying decisions are rational and binary. If that were true, the lowest price or the best product would always win in the end. But we know this isn't how the world works.

Brand Keys, a New York-based brand consulting firm, conducted a 2010 Customer Loyalty Engagement Index. According to an article in *Brandweek*,[9] they polled 33,500 consumers of 518 brands in 71 industry categories.

Brand Keys asked consumers detailed questions about how they relate to brands, both emotionally and rationally. Their findings show a link between brand loyalty and

[9] Noreen O'Leary, *Brandweek*, "Report: Starbucks, Wells Fargo Surge in Customer Loyalty," (January 30, 2010)

profitability, especially given the poor economy. during that time. Robert Pasikoff, founder and president of Brand Keys, said customers want more value for their money, which means they want a strong brand for a good price. "With increased standardization and decreased product differentiation," he said, "a real brand can serve up the value consumers expect."

Pasikoff is quoted as saying we are in the "decade of the brand." In the article, he states, "This particular swing, with real brands becoming more valuable to consumers, is showing up in how they view, compare and, most importantly, buy in key categories."

The takeaway here is that human drivers don't change, whether you're Starbucks or Joe's Coffee Shack.

> Your brand needs to clearly communicate something, connect with customers, and show value in order to compete in a crowded marketplace.

All Markets Have a Brand Need: Proud to be Cheap and Disposable

Now let's look at the flip side of Heather's situation. Sometimes people think brand means "expensive," as in "brand name." High cost and exquisite quality are indeed brand attributes, but you could choose to sell a generic T-shirt or dinnerware that's cheap and disposable, since certain audience segments have a real need for those items. As long as you clearly convey this message in everything you do, you can become known as *the* place to buy inexpensive white T-shirts or the most stylish cheap disposable dinnerware. Doesn't mean there's anything wrong with that. The problem arises when you try to be the expensive, luxurious white T-shirt guy with a beautiful website and high prices. But when people get the product, it's the same old cheap white T-shirt that falls apart after two washings.

The opposite might happen as well: you can have expensive, high-end products or services, but your website looks like a ten year-old designed it, or your clerks are rude and unhelpful. Then you have a *brand consistency* problem, or what we talked about earlier as an *identity crisis*. You're trying to be all things to all people, which means you'll be nothing to no one. Good branding is what enables Nordstrom to make a quality white T-shirt and charge three times as much as Kmart. And the brand promise Nordstrom conveys in everything they do – from their high quality goods to impeccable customer service – makes you trust it will indeed be better quality for the price. Nordstrom clearly and consistently communicates quality and high-end attributes in everything they do, from products to store layout to customer service.

Brand is who you are authentically, for better or worse. Whether you sell picture frames or luxury cars, it means you clearly understand the need you fill, the benefits you provide, and how you differ from the competition – and you walk your talk in everything you do.

Like people, brands can be funny, conservative, quirky, soft, simple, no-frills, or elegant. Markets have all kinds of needs.

That's why well-designed, high-end, hip smartphones sell so well – and so do Snuggies and ShamWow's.

Seattle's Portage Bay Café in the following Brand at Work case study consistently emphasizes "clean food" in all that they do – and they walk their talk by delivering what they say and working with suppliers who align with that brand promise.

||||||||||||||||||||||||||||||||||||||||||||||||||||||||||||||||||||||||||||||||||||||||||||||||||||||||||||||||||||||||||||||||||||

BRAND AT WORK: PORTAGE BAY CAFE

"Eat like you give a damn." That is the tagline – and brand philosophy – of Portage Bay Café (www.portagebaycafe. com), an organic restaurant with three Seattle locations. According to owner John Gunnar, his commitment to selling organic, sustainable, and local food is all about giving customers "clean food." He targets professionals and progressive types who want to feel confident that the food they consume is healthy and clean. "We target people who care about what they're eating and where it comes from," says John. And they do it all with a sense of play and lightheartedness – hence, the unconventional tagline."Our brand is about healthy, clean, progressive living but without taking things too seriously. We like to have fun with our ads, our messages and show that you don't have to be pretentious and uptight to enjoy healthy, clean, local food."

John learned early in his business about the power of focusing his brand on a niche audience and serving them well. He realized back in 1997 when he started with a more standard café that he was trying to be all things to all people. As an organic eater himself, John had an epiphany that he wasn't being authentic with his own business and brand. So he began integrating organics into the menu and raising prices accordingly. This was a huge gamble – but it paid off: he tripled business in a year and a half. John ensured this organic message was pervasive. In order to build the reputation and brand, he placed it on the menus, table tents, everywhere. "Our brand works because I am personally passionate about it," John says. "We go after a niche, but it's one I believe in. You have to believe in your brand and what you are doing."

Obviously, the brand plays a role when sourcing food. John only partners with suppliers that provide organic and sustainable ingredients, trying to buy locally whenever possible. And his focus on professional and progressive people who are willing to spend more to "eat clean" helps him decide on marketing tactics: Portage Bay Café sponsors a lot of sports-oriented events to attract his target demo. John has turned down radio station ads when their listeners were not a good fit. He did, however, advertise with the local NPR station and, true to brand form, created some campy and cheeky ads that conveyed his playful perspective. His strongest marketing tools are word of mouth and turning new customers into loyal returning patrons. "Sometimes, the best testament of our brand value is when people find a bug in their food and are good-natured about us replacing it. They really admire that you walk your talk and provide pesticide-free food right from the source!"

Brand is Not Just a Logo: It's Everything

From this authentic core, your brand can spring forth. Once you can acknowledge how you change people's lives – whether you sell to consumers or to other businesses – you can better understand how to convey that across all of your communications. When I say communications, I mean **every touchpoint you have with people: visual, verbal, and experiential.** Customers see your brand in the visual elements you convey: your logo, website, brochures, and signage. They "hear" your brand in your website copy, live presentations, elevator pitch, and press stories. And they experience your brand through the buying process, how they're treated by customer service, the caliber of your employees, and so on.

Let's take an example. Suppose you sell chic, simple humidors for cigar aficionados. Your ideal customer is someone – perhaps a woman – who loves cigars but doesn't want the humidor to stick out like a sore thumb in her home. Most humidors are bulky and showy objects made of dark, heavy wood. But a whole client base out there likes simple, clean lines in their homes and wants something to go with their décor. The problem you solve for them is to make cigars fit unobtrusively into their stylish homes and lifestyle. "Simple. Clean. Unobtrusive. Chic."

Given this, would you ever design a website with cramped copy, minimal white space, and a confusing array of choices? Would your logo be loud and bold to get noticed? Would your customer service reps sound harried and rushed when answering the phone?

No, no, and no. Your site might be simple to navigate and your colors would represent simple elegance and sophistication, perhaps using white, silver, and black as a contrast to competitors' dark, heavy colors. For your products, you'd show basic color and design options and simple shots of each, with a short description. Your copy tone would be refined and casual – not based on hyperbole and exclamation points. Your call center reps would be courteous, to the point, and knowledgeable. They would efficiently take care of customers without noise or chaos in the background.

This is what it means to live your brand in everything you do. Now every time a customer comes to your website, sees your product, encounters your ads, or calls your sales order line, they have a consistent experience. When you extend your brand beyond the promotional or visual aspects to include policies, hiring decisions, or the like, I call this **operationalizing your brand** You are literally injecting the brand into the DNA of your company and ensuring the entire customer experience, visual *and* experiential, is clear and consistent. And this "brands" (pun intended) your brand into their psyche to occupy the "simple, chic, unobtrusive, clean" space in their brain.

See how much easier all the other decisions become when you know who you are and what you're about? If you don't have a solid brand foundation, your decisions will be random and end up costing you money for nothing.

Brand as Design Guide: Hug a Designer Today

People tend to think designers are magical wizards who can read minds and create intricate, beautiful visuals within an hour. Eager entrepreneurs with hope in their eyes seek out designers to turn visions into reality. They plead, "Make me a logo" or "Build me a website," but offer no direction as to what these items should communicate.

Going to a designer for a logo and website without a Brand Strategy is like handing someone a wad of money and saying, "Go shopping." If you don't say what you need, for whom you're buying, and for what occasion, only a mind-reader would be able to accurately spend that money on what you desire. If you treat a designer this casually, I can see countless revisions and billable hours in your future.

This is an extreme example for effect, but it's what people often do when working with designers. We ask them to communicate something visually without a clear directive on what we want to communicate, and to whom. Or we give them our personal taste: "I love pink" or "I want my logo to be a cat, because I like cats." This is all well and good – and the fun part of owning your own business – but if you haven't thought about your audience and what *they* want and need, you'll have the prettiest website at the party but no one will ask you to dance. Your designer will struggle to visually convey what you're trying to communicate, which will be frustrating to both of you. It's sound business practice to not just hire a good agency, but to be a good client as well.

If you want a funny tagline on your logo, is that because it will resonate with your audience or you personally just like funny taglines? But what if you're a funeral home?

If you're selling to teenagers, should you have a traditional, boring website? Aha! Don't make a false assumption and say no right off the bat. Maybe you do need a simple site. The layout depends on the teens you're trying to attract, what brand promise you offer, and what they need.

Know thy brand, know thy audience: only then can your designer easily create thy logo, website, and brochures. You will also know how to package your products, how to answer the phone, and what your automated email from customer service should say. Any writer you hire can also more easily craft your main messages and tagline.

Bridget Perez, a partner at Tray Creative (www.traycreative.com) is a creative director who helps businesses communicate their brand visually and ensure the designs impact the buying decision. In her experience, color is one of the most important elements of branding. "Sixty percent of the decision to buy a product is based on color," she says. "The brain registers shape first, then color, then content when recognizing or remembering something, like a logo.

Think about a well-known brand, like Target or UPS, then imagine if you saw the Target logo in blue or a UPS truck that was orange ... would you even register it?" Design choices like color, layout, and font can compel the right audience to buy when they are used correctly – or repel your audience from buying when they are not.

We'll explore more about how to apply color in Part 3.

Part 2:
How to Build
Your Brand Strategy

IF YOU HAVE MILLIONS OF DOLLARS and tons of time, you can spend months working with a slick agency to craft your Brand Strategy. They can do primary and secondary research, engage in detailed competitive audits, and try all kinds of messaging and concepts. But most small business owners or non-profit organizations don't have this kind of money or time. You probably want a basic strategy to ensure you're on the right path and thinking about the right things.

The ten questions in this section will help you reach the heart of your Brand Strategy.

This process is especially designed for small business owners, start-up professionals, and non-profit executives who lack big budgets.

Two caveats: One, this book won't tell you the "right" Brand Strategy for your business. As mentioned in Part 1, you need to discover which brand will be most effective for your target customers, as well as the brand promise you can authentically make and consistently deliver to them. The questions will guide you toward personal answers that fit your organization. This process also works for service-oriented businesses and nonprofit agencies – just think of donors or clients instead of customers.

Two, the answers to the ten questions aren't meant to be the exact words you'll use for marketing materials. Your answers will be raw materials you can later shape into website copy, a brochure, or even store signage. Without this foundation, you won't even know how to start writing those external messages.

Your answers to the following ten questions will form the basis of your Brand Strategy. The information you glean from this exercise will save time, money, and frustration on a thousand little business decisions. And if you share these ten answers with a designer or writer, be prepared: they may jump up and hug you. Many designers build time into their project costs to go over these steps with you, so if you can do this heavy lifting on your own – and I believe you can – then you'll save time and money.

You may need to hire a writer for a few hours to help polish your ideas, but you'll already have the bulk of your strategy done. This will be your first step to ensuring the clarity and consistency we talked about in Part 1.

In addition, don't worry about format. Answer these questions however you wish. You can use Word, Excel, or PowerPoint. You might even try the old-fashioned way by writing things down in a notebook. In this exercise, your thought process is much more important than format.

Ten Key Questions to Building Your Brand Strategy

1. How do you describe your company and what you do?
2. What are the product or service package and pricing descriptions?
3. What are the organization's strengths and weaknesses?
4. What are the adjectives and emotions around your brand?
5. Who and where is your audience? What do they look like? What do they read? What groups do they join? How can you find them?

6. What are the main benefits you provide to customers? Why can you make those claims?
7. Who is your competition and how are you different?
8. How do you need to communicate: With current clients/interested parties? With new prospects?
9. What is your company's greatest asset/one unique thing?
10. Metrics: How do we measure success?

Question 1: How do you describe your company and what you do?

Small businesses and start-up firms often try to run before they can walk by dazzling the public with lofty marketing-speak, leaving folks asking, "What is it you actually *do?*" If you can't condense the essence of what you do into one or two crisp sentences, you won't be able to create benefit statements and other brand elements later on. I'd be a millionaire by now if I had a dollar for every time someone at a networking event gets up to talk about their small business, but never bothers clarifying whether they sell a product or a service, or if they operate online versus just a brick and mortar establishment.

What does your business do? Forget the marketing gloss. When it comes right down to it, what product or service do you provide to whom and why should they care?

Before we move on to loftier things like a mission statement or a tagline, you need to have this basic description down cold.

A mighty oak starts as a tiny acorn.

Seems simple, right? But have you ever talked to two employees of the same organization who describe the business in totally different ways? Drives me crazy, too. I find this step is often the most powerful way to clear away the clutter, and it builds a strong brand and messaging base. Just as basketball players start with the fundamentals before they can be the next Michael Jordan, you've got to nail the simple drills before you can tackle the complex plays.

Are you a product or service? Are you a content provider or distributor? Are you only online or do you have a physical shop? Do you plan events or connect people at events? Do you resell a manufacturer's product or make your own? Do you sell wholesale or direct to consumers? You should be able to boil this down to one or two sentences. Here are some examples:

- A manufacturer of athletic footwear, apparel, and equipment for men, women and children
- A provider of women's hair care products and services, online and through salons
- A maker of automobile windows and windshields
- A programmer for small business websites
- A business coach who helps entrepreneurs write business plans
- A non-profit agency that provides shelter, resources, and job training services to the homeless in urban areas

Leave the branding stuff – pithy taglines or the "we guide women down the right path" mission statements – for later. Don't start with tactics before you build the Brand Strategy to support those tactics. "Tactics" include choosing the right marketing messages and taglines.

Another way to approach this question in its simplest form is to adopt the approach of Christopher Flett, Founder of Ghost CEO (www.ghostceo.com) and author of *What Men Don't Tell Women About Business* (2007, Wiley and Sons). Ghost CEO provides leadership development training and business consulting to women business owners. I love Chris's pragmatic, take-no-prisoners style as he helps businesswomen attain success. Chris and his team always ask clients, right off the bat, to describe their business in the following way: "What do you do? Why does it matter? Who cares?" That's it, bottom line. No catch phrases or taglines. Everything else is built upon how clearly you answer this question.

EXERCISE:

Write a basic description of what your organization does and who it serves in an easy-to-understand sentence or two, with no marketing hype. Run this by a few people who know nothing about your business and see if they "get" what you do and for whom you do it.

Question 2: What are the product/service package and pricing descriptions?

Even if they haven't started their business yet, most people have a good idea of what products or services they want to offer and at what price. If you're a writer, do you charge by the hour, by the project, or do you offer a Communication Basics Package that includes five pages of website copy, a company description, press release boilerplate, and a tagline – all for one price? If you're a boutique, do you sell certain products within a given price range? You may need to pull some of this information from your business plan.

We answer this question in a more abstract way than you would on a detailed revenue forecasting model. Why? Because we have a different purpose in mind: brand development. This process assumes the prices you offer have already been vetted within a forecasting model or business planning process and that you aren't losing money on each sale.

I recommend you save the answers to this question, because later on you'll perform a sanity check against the rest of your Brand Strategy. For example, if you go through the entire Brand Strategy process and find your target audience is small business owners, you'll want to be sure your price points are reasonable for this audience, versus multi-million dollar corporations. Or you may find, as some of my clients have, that you *want* to target a certain audience, but you've priced your products or services way out of their reach.

You also need to include pricing in your Brand Strategy because it will eventually contribute to *how* you represent your brand. Will you be the Porsche of your industry? If so, you may need to increase your prices to align with this brand promise. Otherwise, people won't believe in your value. Or do you want to be the Kia of your market? If so, high prices don't align with that image and the target audience who would buy the Kia can't afford you. What good will it do if all of your customer touch points are talking to folks who can't buy from you? You either need to change your prices or alter your brand image. You could position yourself as "Porsche quality at Kia prices," but then you'd have to deliver on that promise – and you might not be bringing in enough revenue to realistically fulfill this for customers, thus leaving a bad taste in their mouths.

In addition, writing down the actual packages or items you offer will help you compare apples to apples when you examine the competition. For example, you might be the only one who offers a unique package in your market. That's a company strength you'll want to emphasize at the end when we put the brand into action in Part 3 of this book.

EXERCISE:

In a table or grid, list each product or service you offer and how much you charge. If you offer packages, note these and write down everything they include. If you're a retail shop or online store with many items, list a representative sample of items and the price ranges for each. For example, a boutique might offer "Casual dresses, ranging from $200 to $500; Jewelry, ranging from $50 to $400."

Question 3: What are your strengths and weaknesses?

Your brand communications should ideally play to your strengths and downplay or address your weaknesses, turning them into positives. By strengths and weaknesses, I'm not referring to your individual products. I'm talking about your business as a whole. Since this is your corporate Brand Strategy, we need to take the macro view on this answer rather than considering individual products. The answers will form the basis of the words you use and the company's overall visual look and feel. You can certainly talk in the aggregate about your product offering ("We're the only distributor of Product X in the region") but avoid a laundry list of specific product strengths and weaknesses. Remember, this exercise will help you focus on overall businesses strengths you want to convey with your company's brand.

What unique things can your business offer? What compelling assets, skills or connections do you have?

What does your business really have going for it? Where is your business vulnerable? Where do you fall down against the competition? You may find some of these answers in your business plan. As a small business owner or founder, you may represent the face of your business: your personal strengths are its strengths. So, a strength can even be YOU. For example, being well-connected in the community gives you an advantage over other businesses. Or do you have unique experience in your background that no one in your space can claim, making you an expert? The founder of Jane Spice (www.janespice.com), one of my clients, has a unique and distinct ethnic heritage and has lived in fantastic "foodie" places like Sydney, Australia and San Francisco, California. This works well for her online spice and recipe blog. Her personal experience and story is a brand advantage that gives her a leg up on other blogs and eCommerce sites that do the same thing. In the Brand at Work case study below, we see how one woman's unique professional background is her main brand strength and, by communicating it throughout her company's messages and operations, helps her business stand out.

BRAND AT WORK: MAJOR MOM

Who better to get your home or office in tip top order than a former U.S. Air Force Major? That unique brand differentiator helps Angela Cody-Rouget, CPO (Chief Professional Organizer) of Major Mom (www.MajorMom. biz) stand out from hundreds of bland, look-alike professional organizing companies. Major Mom's key brand attributes are fun, affordability, and professionalism. And Angela walks her talk. She has two decades of training in order management, serving in the U.S. Air Force for 18 years and eventually attaining the rank of Major. She embraces and thrives in orderly environments. The company mission is "to restore order and serenity to a client's home and office so they will experience the joy of living and working in organized and beautifully arranged environments." The mission is bigger than just "putting stuff away." Angela is out to restore peace in the home and bring families together.

This efficient and professional brand promise is the basis for every decision, from employees' unique camo and T-shirt uniforms to an efficient hiring process mapped out on their website. "Each time we create forms to use on the job or train our staff, we're thinking about brand consistency," Angela says. "We create our HR, PR, Customer Care, and Sales Systems with our brand in mind. Consistency will help us build a national company."

Running her company like a well-oiled machine assures clients that Angela can indeed get their own homes and offices in order. This consistency is further articulated in a new recruit training academy and six-month apprenticeship that ensures all employees (not just Angela) will adopt and live the brand values.

Angela's distinct mission, vision, and brand values are clearly and consistently communicated across every brochure, ad, website page, and even their voicemail message. These values consciously guide business decisions. In one case, Angela turned down a PR opportunity on an influential radio and TV personality's show because his approach and demeanor didn't align with Major Mom's brand and values. She has also turned down a partnership opportunity with another organizing company that focused on "hauling junk" rather than her mission of making your home your treasure. Having such a strong brand that breaks the mold enabled Angela to extend beyond Colorado to California and Texas. She's well on her way to achieving her vision to be the most recognized and respected organizing firm in the United States and the world.

A weakness could be "It's a crowded market of many look-a-likes" or "I lack start-up capital so I have to charge upfront for services." Be honest with yourself. Being modest might cause you to miss a valuable opportunity to emphasize the good things and downplay the bad.

Many start-ups could stand to spend a day with key corporate stakeholders, or even a select group of their customers, to figure out what makes them tick and how they could improve. If you're an established business with customers, ask them what they think. Why did they buy from you? What drew them to you? What do they think you are lacking? Customers are a gold mine of information for businesses. Don't be afraid. Customers who like you will want you to succeed and they won't mind being part of that process. You can further cement your relationship with them by bringing them into this branding process. Send them a quick survey online via Emma (www. myemma. com) or SurveyMonkey (www.surveymonkey. com) to glean this information. Just remember to ask them to be honest and offer some type of incentive, such as a complimentary service, discount coupon or a free coffee card, in exchange for their valuable time.

If that's too complicated, then send an email or letter to a select group of customers and ask for their opinion. You might try polling a customer who made a return or bought from you once and never again, just to get juicy feedback. Keep the survey under ten questions to respect their time, and try not to ask leading questions like, "Do you like our amazingly low prices that offer real value for the money?" Articles and videos are available on the web to help you craft a good survey – just type in "Effective Surveys" to Bing or Google.

I once worked on a Brand Strategy project for a non-profit organization that wanted to increase donations and community awareness about their services. As part of this work, we interviewed a representative sample of stakeholders, including employees, clients, donors, and board members to get a sense of their brand perception and what they felt the organization was doing right and wrong. But the non-profit went a step further and had us interview clients who had a negative experience. This yielded some of the most profound insights and perspectives for us. While happy folks talked about the brand in terms of what the company intended to communicate, the unhappy folks showed us gaps between brand promise and the brand reality.

Because brand lives in the mind of your customers, you need to take some of the bad with the good in order to make improvements. The executive director knew that for every one of these unhappy folks willing to talk, at least ten others had the same viewpoint but didn't speak up – they just walked away. Worse, they virally spread the word about their negative experience.

Based on the information, we were able to revise their brand messaging and offer operational recommendations about the organization's training, client care, and communication processes that were out of whack with the brand promise they were touting.

Finding out why people don't like you can be even more powerful than finding out why they do.

> *EXERCISE:*
>
> Create a two-column list with one column titled Strengths and the other Weaknesses. Start listing quick bullet points about you and your business at a high level (not product by product) for each column. Got a great location? Dub that a strength. Are you brand new in town and lack a strong community network to promote your business? Make that a weakness. Do you as the founder or CEO have a unique educational, work, or personal history that your competitors lack? List that as a strength. If you're small and your competitors are large, this could be a weakness when it comes to buying power and awareness, but it could be a strength: you might be more flexible when working with clients and offer more personalized service. In that case, you'd list your size under both columns.

Question 4: What are the adjectives and emotions around your brand?

This is the fun stuff. If you think at all about brand, this is probably the task that most often comes to mind. The adjectives, images, or emotions around your brand are also known as *brand attributes*. What descriptive words come to mind when you think about your company and its offerings? How do you want others to see you? Do you want to be professional, serious, and trusted, or do you want to be playful and sassy? Do you want to be formal or casual?

> Decide which space in customers' minds you want to occupy; in which mental file drawer you want them to tuck you away.

Having these listed will help a designer see your vision and create an appropriate logo or website. And these words will also educate a writer on what tone or word choices are best for your marketing messages and website copy.

You can also leverage the brands of people or characters to describe your own brand attributes. If I describe a brand as Audrey Hepburn, you instantly get a picture of grace, femininity, elegance, and beauty without me saying all of that. So don't be afraid to borrow images from famous people or historical personalities in your Brand Strategy to help convey your vision. I once had a technology client who wanted to be the Anderson Cooper of his niche space: young, tech-savvy, trusted, intelligent and professional. Analogies are a useful tool to help you judge the fit of a marketing program or to describe what you want your designer to do with your website. Another great way to do this is by comparing your organization to other items that have brands, as we discussed in Part 1: holidays, places, TV shows, movies, or fictional characters. Are you New York City or Santa Fe? *The Deadliest Catch* or *The View*? Romantic comedy or crime thriller?

Small businesses and start-ups tend to list way too many brand attributes, to the point that they can't possibly represent *all* of them. I recommend that clients brainstorm everything that comes to mind first, and then go back and cut that list in half. Then cut it in half again and repeat until they're left with the most crucial five to seven adjectives, images, or phrases. As we stated in Part 1, trying to be everything to everyone will result in being nothing to no one. Focus on what's most important.

This short list may lead to a positioning statement such as, "I want my business to be the Rolls Royce of car washes." You may not end up putting that verbatim description before the public, but it goes along way toward helping a designer create an appropriate logo, or helping you decide whether an ad in a particular magazine might tarnish the brand image you want to convey.

Question 5: Who and where is your audience? How can you find them?

This is the **single most important aspect to a strong Brand Strategy.** If you don't know your audience intimately and make them real, you'll be shooting at a moving target. Often, business owners say, "Everyone is my target audience." They're afraid to exclude a particular group, because in certain situations, that person *could* feasibly buy something from them. Yes, in the big picture, anyone may buy anything, but you need to focus your attention and dollars on the ones *most likely* to buy. We aren't talking about *to whom you're willing to sell*: we're talking about where you'll spend your limited time and money on attracting the lowest hanging fruit.

Think about your *ideal customer*, not your average customer.

"Average" will dilute your answer too much, leading to generic, vanilla communication that won't appeal to anyone. I always tell clients, "When you try to be everything to everyone, you end up being nothing to nobody." It's akin to throwing a dart at a dartboard that has no red bullseye in the center, but is painted all white: how will you know where to aim, or if you're even close to the center?

Pretend you have a group of one hundred people in a room and can pick the dream person who best represents your ideal client or customer. Who would that be? Or select an example from your best customers and base the profile on him or her.

For example, you can say you sell to women, but that category is much too broad. Do you mean a grandma or a newlywed? City girl or country girl? Married or single? Parent or not? Working or stay-at-home? There are many different women out there, with different buying needs, interests and styles. Generally speaking, a progressive 24-year-old single graphic designer in Los Angeles may have different tastes and needs than a conservative 56-year-old, stay-at-home mother of four in Duluth. Flesh out as much detail for this ideal customer as you can. Give her a name and an occupation. Tell me where she works (if she works), how she gets there, what she reads, what she watches on TV (does she watch TV?), where she shops, how she dresses, and where she gets her news and information. To what clubs or groups does she belong? What does she do for fun? All of this will help later on when you invest in marketing tactics, because you'll be able to see which ideas will get in front of your targets and which are a waste of time and money. It will also help you discover unexpected ways to reach your audience.

A past client in financial services came to work with me on the Brand Strategy for his new business. He had no website, no materials, nothing: this is one of *my* ideal client segments. But he did have a script for a TV ad he'd written and eagerly hoped to use one day. His ad was good, but while going through the ten step process we discovered his ideal client was too busy balancing her own successful firm and her family to even watch TV. If she did watch, she recorded programs and zapped past the commercials, so investing in a local TV ad would have been a waste of money. By doing the ideal customer exercise, however, we uncovered a channel he had never thought about: radio. His ideal client commutes to work in her car for at least 20 minutes a day and she most likely listens to NPR. So investing in a radio ad on the local NPR station was much more effective than a local TV spot.

Another client figured out her ideal customer frequents coffee shops more than most people. Even though her business didn't seem to jump out and scream "Advertise in coffee shops" she realized well-worded postcards for people to pick up and take back to their offices would be just the thing. They could then log on to her site from the office, or even right at the coffee shop, because her ideal customers held meetings there. Unless you do this creative exercise, you may never discover unique little ways to get in front of your best potential customers.

On the flip side, this exercise also helps you avoid spending money on marketing that doesn't work. NASCAR is hugely popular with certain types of people and draws millions to their events, but do you think Nordstrom spends money marketing there to reach its ideal client? Would Harley Davidson advertise at a tennis match? Knowing your customer intimately will help you avoid the temptation to invest in just any marketing opportunity or partnership that crosses your path. You'll have a perfect benchmark to judge the worth of advertising campaigns.

Many clients are afraid to eliminate a potential group of customers. They say, "But I could sell to this person or this person, or that person. And one time, this one type of customer did buy from me, so maybe I should be marketing to that whole segment. I can't leave any of them out because they're all potential sales." The reality is that you only have so much money to spend and so much time. You want to go deep on the activities that get the most traction, not pursue a broad range of one-time activities that get you nowhere. The broad range approach is akin to skipping a stone over water: you'll hit a lot of points, but won't make a big impression in any of them.

Don't be afraid of this exercise – you'll end up catching ancillary people in your net even if you don't target them, and it's not like you won't take their money if they don't fit your ideal customer criteria. This is not about to whom you will sell (although if you are a service business, it could serve as a great checklist for determining which clients you will or will not take on.) This is about deciding where to focus your limited time, energy, and budget for the greatest impact. Think of it as a fashion designer does: who will be your "brand muse? In the following Brand at Work case study, you can see how CasaQ carved out a unique focus instead of trying to do it all – and how this specific expertise has made them a sought-after partner.

\\\

BRAND AT WORK: CasaQ

Darlene Tenes used to sell imported décor items from Mexico. But when she wanted to find home products with a Latino flair, there was nothing on the market or at gift shows that met her quality and authenticity standards. Sensing a need, Darlene decided to design culturally significant products herself that reflected her own lifestyle and values.

She created CasaQ (www.casaq.com), a San Jose, California-based Hispanic lifestyle company dedicated to providing unique products, services, and content geared toward people who embrace the Latino culture. CasaQ is focused on inspiring others to learn, teach, and share this rich culture. "I am very particular about getting the details of the designs and the history correct on all of my products," Darlene says.

CasaQ could have gone beyond Latino-inspired products but Darlene stays true to her core brand promise, which ends up resonating with folks outside that demographic. "CasaQ is about sharing and preserving our culture and in doing so, it creates a bond with other people who have similar traditions and customs, many of which have been shared or merged with other cultures." Forty percent of their retail sales and ninety percent of their wholesale buyers are not Latino.

CasaQ is based on the things Darlene authentically finds most important in life: faith, culture, family, and of course, food. The "Q" stands for "*querida*" which means "loving" or "darling". And Casa Querida means "a loving home," which is exactly what she has in mind when designing her ornaments. Simply using the Q in the company name helps the company remain memorable to non-Spanish speakers and thus easier to find online.

This "loving home" brand value extends to trusting customers like family. They gladly replace or refund for broken items, no questions asked. And if CasaQ makes an order mistake, they send a handwritten note and small gift. "My employees need to have a passion for history and culture so they can be excited about the products and mission of the company no matter what their position. That's part of being a team or a family," says Darlene.

Living this brand mission inside and out has helped CasaQ attract some big accounts. They design ornaments for Grupo Modelo, the Mexican beer manufacturer and distributor, who approached the company because of their focus and understanding of Latino culture. "Other manufacturers may have slapped their logo on an ornament or created a copy of the beer bottle but it wasn't in our DNA to do so," says Darlene. "I personally sketched and designed ornaments that celebrated the popular Latino culture and incorporated their logo or bottle into the design." That focus and passion for the culture has helped CasaQ get into major museums and exclusive gift stores because buyers trust the knowledge and care that is put into each product. Next up: a line of kitchen textile products are being added to the collection next year.

///

My husband is another great example. He's an avid video gamer, and we own a Wii, a PSP, and an XBOX. He is in his mid-30s, a successful tech company executive with a wife, a mortgage, and a dog. Do you really think the XBOX team is spending money and time specifically trying to reach his target profile? Probably not. They're going after younger, single guys who have fewer obligations and more gaming time. In fact, I see their ads on networks like Fuse or G4 that target such a demographic. But this doesn't mean their messages don't resonate with someone like my husband. After all, he watches those networks occasionally, right?

He still gets "caught in the net" because the products and brand promise appeal to him. Will XBOX specifically devote dollars and time to reaching a whole segment of people like my husband? Maybe, if they get enough traction from it (and word is that they actually will start targeting people like my husband as one unique customer profile.) But the more important point is, their ideal customer profile guides the company on where and how to target their brand and marketing dollars. If they catch others in that net, that's just gravy.

Companies the size of Microsoft use different customer profiles for each product group. They sell both consumer and business products, after all, and *every* brand and product in their portfolio doesn't appeal to *every* audience type.

Recently, I read that Hyundai is creating a line of cars especially for folks who are moving back to the city from the suburbs. According to the article, "Their ideal customer is a couple in their late 50s who have traded in their sprawling suburban home for a nicely appointed condo in an up-and-coming city, like Seattle. They have sold off one of their two cars and are decluttering their lives. They socialize, eat well and live for new experiences."[10]

Now, many of these traits have nothing to do with buying a car, and I'm sure if someone in their 20s who doesn't eat well and lives with mom and dad wanted to buy a car, Hyundai would still sell one to him. The point is that even companies with millions to spend on marketing and branding do this ideal customer exercise.

Defining your ideal audience also helps with pricing and packaging (Question 3), as we previously stated. You can ensure that what you offer and how you price it is consistent with your ideal customer. You'd be surprised how often the two do not match up initially. For example, saying your ideal customer is a "soloprenuer" but then pricing your products too high for his limited budget.

---

[10] Joseph B. White, *The Wall Street Journal,* "Dude, Where's My Car?" (October 28, 2009)

Write a one-page character profile of your ideal customer. Try not to create more than three different profiles for now. Give this person a name, an age, and a marital status. Tell me where they work, what they watch on TV, what they do for fun, how much money they make, what a typical day is like for them, how do they commute, which groups or associations they belong to, what magazines they read, and anything else that comes to mind. Be as specific and creative as possible. This will help you see new ways to get your brand in front of the people who matter most.

Question 6: What are the main benefits you provide and why can you make those claims?

Here's a common challenge for small businesses and start up firms: They often become so involved with daily operations that they only think about what they're selling. They're unable to look at their business with fresh eyes, from a customer's viewpoint. When asked what benefit they provide or why someone should buy from them, they fall back on a product or service description. "The benefit is that we build websites cheaply," or "we sell organic yoga clothes." But how does the customer see you? What value do they receive from using your services or purchasing items from your firm? What problem do they have that your product or service solves?

A simple exercise will help you decide if you've landed on the benefit. Name a feature of your company and ask yourself: "So why does that matter?" If you can keep drilling down and asking, "So what?" then you know you haven't reached the benefit yet. Here's an example:

"We sell yoga clothes made from organic materials" (So why should organic materials matter to me?)

"Because the clothes are made of natural, breathable fibers" (So why do natural, breathable fibers matter to me?)

"Because you can move more freely and comfortably in the clothes" (So why does that matter to me?)

"You can get more health benefits from your yoga practice if you have comfortable clothes that enable you to move more easily." (Bingo!)

See how I went from talking about "What We Do" to "What the Clothes Do" to finally "What you – the customer – get?" Many businesses simply tout *what they sell* (features) but don't explain *why anyone should care* (benefits).

Ideally, your features serve as proof for why you can make a certain benefit claim. For example, "side-impact air bags" is a feature; "Keeps you safe in a crash" is the benefit. If you're a yoga studio, "we offer 5 types of yoga classes for all levels" is a feature; "Find just the right class that fits your skill level so you get more out of each class" is the benefit.

If you don't have a good handle on how to verbalize the benefits you provide, you won't be able to build a brand that resonates both consciously and subconsciously with customers. They won't form an attachment to you as a way to make their lives better. The lack of benefits will leave all your marketing messages flat.

Here's a marketing secret: As buyers, we're all selfish beings. Why shouldn't we be? After all, we're spending *our* money. So I ask, "What's in it for me? What does your product or service do for me and why should I believe you?"

In marketing terms, the answers to "What does your product or services do for me?" yield *benefits*. The answers to "Why should I believe you?" yield *proof points or features*.

The above is true whether you sell to consumers or businesses. Many B2B (business-to-business) technology start-ups revert to spewing out a laundry list of features and functions when trying to make sales. They wonder why this doesn't work. They say, "Showing more features proves to the prospect that our product is way ahead of the competition." But that isn't how it works. You may have the best widgets in the world, but if I can't understand how your product solves my problem, then I just don't care. The features are only proof points that should support a greater benefit. What does the state-of-the-art, advanced widget-producing technology with customized interfaces and 900 gigs of cloud-computing space actually *do* for me or my company? How will it solve my problems? Yes, a technical buyer will care about what's behind the curtain (the features), but only *after* he's hooked by what he'll get out of the product overall. And besides, if his job is riding on the decision he makes, one of the benefits could be that he'll look like a rock star and get promoted for choosing your safe, reliable, fast-performing product.

On the flip side of just listing proof points or features, some small businesses tout benefits without proof points. This is useless, because no one will believe your claims. As you build a brand promise you must be able to back it up. Benefits like "low cost" and "best quality" are generic, and you absolutely must prove why you're able to say this. Making the claim isn't enough to build a strong brand in the customer's mind. You'll have to fulfill the brand promise, after all. Remember, brand isn't just what you say it is, or what your visuals show, it's how the customer's actual experience aligns with that promise.

Another way to work out the benefits customers get from your products or services is to uncover their problems first and then focus on how your business solves them. You can offer them a vision for what their lives can be like if they have your product or service so they will want to learn more. "Too many companies describe their products to customers by explaining features, "says Matt Heinz of Heinz Marketing (www.heinzmarketing.com) a consulting agency that helps businesses with their sales and go-to-market strategies. "That's a mistake, especially at the front of the conversation and sales cycle. To gain the customer's attention, you have to speak in terms of benefits. Don't talk about the How and What. Address the Why."

Let's take an example. Joe's firm offers customers new websites built on the WordPress platform, or he transitions HTML-based websites over to this platform. This is what he does or sells (Question #1.) But the *benefit* Joe provides is a low-cost way to get a high-quality website. He solves the customer dilemma that "good websites cost too much to build and maintain." Joe has a few proof points (or features) to back up this low-cost claim: one, he works remotely from his home office, giving him low overhead; two, he uses pre-built templates and customizes them, rather than spending hours coding new sites from scratch; and three, Joe uses WordPress, an easy-to-use website platform, so his customers can update the sites on their own, rather than paying a programmer to make changes. Joe's high-quality proof points are that he personally customizes each website until it's exactly what the client wants, and the templates he uses are the best WordPress has to offer in terms of flexibility and support.

Why should people buy from you? What problem do you solve? Why should they care or believe you? The answers to this step form the basis of a full-blown messaging platform, and they'll help you create the elevator pitch that you'll learn more about in Part 3 of the book.

EXERCISE:

Compose a list of three to five main benefits your business provides, from a customer's point of view. Think about what customers ultimately gain by using your products or services. Do you increase their profits, lower their costs, make them more beautiful, boost self-confidence, preserve precious memories, or reduce stress?

For each main benefit, create a bulleted list of three proof points that show why you can make that claim. Try to be concise with your language – don't ramble on for multiple sentences about each benefit.

Question 7: Who is your competition? How are you different?

Creating a snapshot of your competition and the reasons people might buy from them is always a smart move. This way, your brand promise and messaging can clearly address how you're different and why customers should come to you instead. Many business owners can verbally explain to me why they're a better alternative than the competition, but that information doesn't come across clearly in their messaging or the brand itself. Branding is all about differentiating your business from the other options customers have. This question seems easy if business owners have a direct competitor. But I challenge you to think of competition in a broader sense, as your customers might. What else competes for the dollars they might spend with you? If you're a website designer, then competition is more than just other designers; it could be hosting services that offer DIY templates and website authoring tools (i.e., GoDaddy).

In the software industry, the biggest competitor may not be another software firm offering the exact same solution, but a customer who opts to build their own custom solution in house from scratch rather than buy a packaged product. This is also known as "Build vs. Buy."

Other competition might be internal priorities that compete for the money a customer might spend on your product or service.

> Knowing what you're up against will help you craft messaging that speaks directly to this issue and enables you to say why you're the best alternative or the best use of the budget dollars.

Competition can be cyclical or time-based as well. Pretend you own a flower shop. Yes, your competitors are other florists in the area, but what about around Valentine's Day or Mother's Day? During those times, a florist might be competing with other unique businesses who are also trying to get their hands on the customer's discretionary funds. Rick, for example, knows he's going to buy something for his wife on Valentine's Day. He has a pool of money set aside for a gift. Rick could choose to spend that money with you, the florist, or he could go to the chocolate shop or the jewelry store. For those special events, several other business types compete with you even though you don't offer the same products. Normally, if someone wants chocolate, they aren't going to look for it in a flower shop or jewelry store, so these businesses aren't always in competition. But during Valentine's Day season, any place that Rick can spend the money he set aside is now your competition. If you want Rick to shop with you, find a way to communicate why your flowers are the best gift choice.

EXERCISE:
Create a list of your competitors, including direct competition and the indirect competition mentioned above. For each competitor, list bullet points of what they provide. Be brief. Then, list why you're a better alternative and how what you offer is different. For this exercise, we can start to look back on the other questions we've answered so far, such as benefits and strengths. You may find those items are also differentiators for you to tout, vis a vis your competition. Knowing how to clearly position yourself against your competitors will help you craft messaging *and* create a visual brand identity that separates you from the pack – like Best Friends general store does in the Brand at Work case study that follows.

BRAND AT WORK: BESTFRIENDS GENERAL STORE

How can a dog parent resist a company that has literally gone to the dogs? BestFriends General Store (www.best friendsgeneralstore.com) is an online dog toy land run by Betsy the Farm Dog and her brother, Norman. These canine owners "run" the business with Candy and Dean Blakeslee, their human parents.

The company's mission is to offer a great selection of quality toys, yummy treats, costumes, and gifts that benefit dogs and promote positive reinforcement. The brand focuses on fun and entertainment, and all communications are written from the dogs' point of view. Product selections are based on items Norman and Betsy would actually use. The dogs write the email newsletters and the toys are approved by them.

Owners Candy and Dean are even listed as second fiddles to the dogs on the website as "their mom/dad and assistant." Candy was surprised no other competitors were using this brand approach when she first started, and she's convinced it's the key to their success. "We would not be in existence if we'd had a normal dog store brand," she says. Because of their amusing tone, commitment to quality, and their ability to offer hard-to-find items, they tend to attract down-to-earth dog owners who would never want to buy pet coats or faux-diamond studded collars. Candy is all about offering quality products that help dogs through positive reinforcement. This mission carries over to supporting local animal shelters and causes.

Their brand mission influences the type of people they hire as well as the products they carry. They've turned down products that could be profitable, but are unhealthy or cause aggressive behaviors. The brand influences packaging as well. Shipments are addressed to "Attention Lucky Dog" and come with dog treats inside, because "every package should be a happy package." When the company makes an error, the customer receives a letter from Betsy and Norman, saying, "Thank you for your patience with our mom and dad. We are trying to train them." This brand differentiator soothes customers and builds rapport – and doesn't cost them an extra dime. After all, who can say no to those faces?

Question 8: How do you communicate with current customers and new prospects?

If you're starting a business from scratch, this one might be a bit loose at the beginning, but remember the Brand Strategy is a living document you can refer back to over time and continue to update. For those of you who already have a business up and running, how are you communicating with your audiences? If your answer is "I'm not really sure," then you already know you have a problem. Branding is about a two-way communication with your customers. If you have no way to talk to them, and more importantly, listen to them, your brand will never grab their loyalty.

You may have answers like "our website" or "marketing postcards." That's okay – list every communication vehicle you have with them, even if it is one-way communication. List your ads, events, catalogs, press releases – all of these are communication vehicles. But also list things like eNewsletters, blogs, automatic email order confirmations, and Twitter if those are mechanisms you use. All your "people interactions" are communication vehicles and branding opportunities as well: store clerks, call center representatives, and your office receptionist.

Now, you can go back to your ideal audience profile and compare notes. How *should* you be communicating with them? Where are they, what information do they need, and which vehicles do they prefer? Which vehicles will they actually pay attention to? Are you spending countless hours on Twitter right now, but your ideal customer profile says your best customers don't even use Twitter? Do you mail an expensive printed newsletter each month, but your customers prefer to get all their communication via email? Do your customers even need a newsletter? This step is important, because you need to consciously compare your communication vehicles with your ideal audience's needs and habits and see if they fit together. Many business owners and start-ups just go out, guns blazing, with a laundry list of tactics. They say, "I need a blog, I need a Facebook fan page," without stopping to think if this is the best use of their time and money. Not every business needs a blog or a newsletter.

Why would you spend time and money on communication vehicles that get you nowhere?

As for acquiring new customers, how can you reach prospects that aren't in your database?

> Take notice if you're treating existing customers and new prospects as one homogenous audience group – they are not.

Sometimes business owners decide to launch customer acquisition programs to a list that includes existing customers. That doesn't make sense, does it? Existing customers and new customers have different needs and a different relationship with you. One group knows you exist and has experienced your brand; the other may not have any clue who you are. So try and treat these groups as two separate audiences. Many brand elements will apply to both, like your visual identity or your product quality, for example. But maybe you need two sections on your website with different benefits and messages: one for existing customers and one for "newcomers." Maybe a discount offer will work for happy, existing customers to get them to purchase again, but you might need a free trial for new customers so they can get a taste of your products. Again, go back to your ideal customer profile.

This question also helps you see if too much of your communication is one-way.

> What mechanisms do you need to put in place for customers to interact with you, offer feedback, or tell you what they want?

Are you delivering any surveys with incentives for folks to respond back? Are you effectively building a tribe or interactive community that can get word-of-mouth going for you? This is where social media can be very helpful –

but again, only if your ideal customer is engaged with social media. Otherwise, it's a waste of time.

EXERCISE:

Create two columns and list all communication vehicles to existing customers on one side, and all vehicles to new prospects on the other. Consider things like ads, website copy, flyers, newsletters, events, and the like. See if there's 100 percent overlap – this may mean you're lumping current customers and prospects together instead of communicating relevant messages to each group. Compare this list back against your ideal customer profile to ensure these vehicles are the best ways to get in front of them, or if you need an alternative plan.

Question 9: What is your company's greatest asset or "One Unique Thing"?

We've talked a lot about benefits and differentiators in the steps above.

> Many small businesses and startups often have at least one differentiator or asset that no other competitor can claim.

This unique asset rises to the top in terms of customer importance and the ability to distance from the pack. This could be something you keep coming back to over and over. If so, you want to identify it and hang your brand's hat on it, visually and verbally. What is that *one thing* that sets you apart? Go back to your strengths and weaknesses or your competitive differentiators and see if one thing uniquely defines you above all else.

For some small businesses, proprietary technology enables customers to do something in a way no one else can. Another business might be the only distributor of a certain top-quality wine within the region. Still others might offer the greatest product selection under the sun in their category – and if they don't have what you're looking for in-store, they can find it for you anywhere in the world. Finally, your greatest asset could be "You." If you as the founder have a unique set of educational qualifications or life experiences, that could be what sets you apart and what you'll want to emphasize with visual and verbal branding.

A client of mine, Andrea Rae of Alinga Bodywork (www. alingabodywork.com), is a massage therapist and energy worker. Dozens of therapists in the Seattle area talk about the same things: serenity, relaxation, and pampering. But Andrea is an outspoken Australian who was an occupational therapist for years, giving her a strong grounding in modern medicine and physical therapy. Her traditional work experience, combined with her pragmatic personality and open mind, give her a unique brand. Her work focuses on delivering results and getting people "unstuck" both physically and mentally, not just on feeling good. So, in her branding we play up her Australian personality and her pragmatic approach of "pampering with purpose." Her background, both educational and personal, is the single most important differentiator she brings to the table. It makes her stand out from everyone else who's selling the same thing. This brand promise yielded a new tagline as well as a newly designed visual identity based on earthy, grounded colors, Aboriginal art and her sassy personality.

If you can't boil your single greatest asset down to one thing no one else can say, you need to put more thought into your positioning, your product mix, or your audience.

EXERCISE:

Review your strengths and your competitive differentiators from the previous questions, as well as your customer benefits. Write down the single greatest asset of your business. What is the top item that will put your offerings in a unique market position? What is the one claim no one else can make in your market space? What unique asset benefits your customers the most and helps you stand out?

Question 10: Metrics: How do you measure success?

Unlike some marketers, I love metrics and they don't scare me at all. I love seeing if something worked or did not. Branding is a little bit gut feel, a little bit art, a little bit timing, and a whole lot of intentional, focused activity and that activity can be measured over time through all the different tactics you employ.

Ultimately, we're all after the same metric: more sales. But not all marketing activities are meant to produce the same goals.

> You have to make your way to "more sales" in small, incremental steps, rather than a giant leap. People won't necessarily buy from you the first time they come in contact with you.

Different aspects of your marketing plan help to move prospects along towards that larger goal. A former manager of mine once termed this, "Taking prospects down a journey." But it all starts with that strong Brand Strategy and promise.

The steps to get to a sale are often called "the sales and marketing cycle." Before customers buy from you, they need to pass through three other phases. For inexpensive "at the cash register" impulse buys such as chewing gum, it may only take someone thirty seconds to go from the first to the last stage. But most other businesses need a bit longer lead time to get a prospect through these phases. Some high-tech software companies have complex cycles that take six to twelve months. The sales and marketing cycle defines the stages a prospective customer goes through when considering you:

- I know you exist,
- I seek more information about you and your product or service,
- I short-list or trial your product or service (either physically or mentally),
- I am ready to buy from you.

As depicted in the figure below, marketers will often call these phases:

- Awareness
- Education
- Consideration or Evaluation
- Purchase

For each phase, put yourself in the prospective customer's shoes and visualize them interacting with you in various ways. Are they driving in their car when the need for your product arises, or will they do extensive web research when buying such a thing? Do they first see your product at a trade show? What would they need when they leave your booth in order to move into the next phase? For each phase of the cycle, the customer has different information needs, so you must plan your marketing activities accordingly. Effective branding and messaging at each phase can also help move them along faster. What do they need to see and hear from you to move down the path?

Different marketing activities correspond to each phase of the cycle, and branding has a role in all of them.

As we discussed, brand informs all your marketing activities, but one of the most important roles brand can play is to get your prospects through the Awareness phase. If your brand is so clear and concise it gets their attention, then you're on your way.

The Brand provides the "air cover" necessary to make all your other marketing activities effective.

Once you establish the brand, you now have a relationship with the prospect that opens the door to promotions, direct marketing offers and the like to move them down the path to purchase. It's a numbers game: the more interest you can generate at the beginning of this funnel with a strong brand, the more sales you get out the other side. Just remember that brand must consistently carry through their entire experience or they will abandon "the journey."

When embarking on either a new business or rebranding an existing one, you can still assign metrics to see if you're gaining traction and actually moving people in the right direction. Once you design your new look and feel, implement your new messaging, build your revamped website, or clarify your offerings and benefits, what will you measure? Before someone can buy from you, they have to know you exist and interact with you. You can measure whether or not their interest is going up. You can look at both quantitative statistics, such as website visits, newsletter signups, or in-store visitors. Equally important are qualitative data, such as an increase in positive customer comments, more local "buzz" as a result of press mentions, or a general uptick in referral business.

Metrics don't have to be scary and they aren't always "number of products sold." Remember, it depends on what your brand or marketing plan includes and which phase the tactics you use are addressing. Metrics can be "website visitors" or "store visitors." Eventually, it does all boil down to sales, but again, remember that different marketing tactics have different goals as you move a prospect down the path to purchase. They can't just skip from A straight to Z. A press release could have a metric of "number of press hits achieved or articles mentioned," because you're trying to get the word out. That awareness may be a new prospect's first step on their journey to a sale with you, which you won't know until much later.

Soliciting and measuring feedback should be a constant activity, even if it's a simple question to a loyal customer such as, "Joan, what do you think of our new store layout or signage?" This way you know if your branding and messaging are going in the right direction.

Have goals in mind before you embark on your brand creation or revamping efforts. This is key to any marketing activity, but especially important when working on your Brand Strategy. What are you trying to achieve? What are your goals? Why are you rebranding now?

Your goals may be as simple as getting twenty new customers a month or gaining three local newspaper press mentions this quarter. If you're rebranding to change perceptions or reposition your company, measure your success by doing a "before" survey, and then an "after" survey three months after you implement your new brand activities. Track and analyze social media chatter with tools like www. socialmention.com to gauge how people are talking about you. If you're launching a newsletter as part of your branding efforts, do you have a monthly goal in mind for subscriber growth? Maybe you're branding your company in a certain way because you have your eye on a specific company with whom you want to partner. The success of the branding effort could be that this partner finally comes knocking after ignoring your calls for years.

EXERCISE:

Come up with five to ten metrics you will measure to ensure your Brand Strategy, and ultimately your marketing plan, is working effectively. Remember, these can be quantitative or qualitative. It's actually a good idea to use some of both, so you should record important anecdotal or general feedback you receive. Make your metrics realistic but time-based if you can, such as "20 new newsletter signups each month" or "50 attendees to each monthly wine tasting event." You can have one of the metrics be a sales number if you like, such as "Generate $2 million in revenue this quarter," but keep that as your ultimate objective – the one to which all your branding and marketing activities, with their individual goals, will lead. Try to keep your brand goals more aligned to increasing visibility, awareness or visits. For each customer, knowing about you and understanding what you offer is the first step required for an eventual purchase.

Putting it All Together

At this point, you should have ten answers to all the questions above. You may need to go back and forth between some of these and revise your answers to earlier questions as you discover more about who you are and what you offer. For example, you may find your prices don't align with your ideal customer target, so you'll need to go back and tweak this.

> The Brand Strategy is a dynamic document that lives and breathes.

It will refresh over time as you learn more about your customers, as your market changes, or as you adapt your offerings. While your core mission and values may stand the test of time, your brand expression, offerings, and differentiators will evolve over the life of your business. That's why you'll want to have solid answers to these brand questions – so you can start working smarter, not harder, and building a clear, consistent promise across all customer touch points. You want to ensure that you feel good about your benefits, your differentiators, your brand attributes and your ideal customer before you go any further with marketing. As stated earlier, the Brand Strategy will form the foundation for all your other marketing and even operational decisions, so it should be in a stable state.

Whether you've done the exercise in Word, PowerPoint, Excel, or even hand-written in a notebook, you'll want to use this information to influence all your business decisions. In Part 3 we'll discuss how to apply this Brand Strategy. If you completed these exercises, give yourself a pat on the back: you've come farther in creating a Brand Strategy than many other business owners, thus increasing your chances for success.

Part 3:
Applying the Brand Strategy

NOW YOU HAVE A PRETTY LITTLE document with the answers to ten vital questions about your business. You've fleshed out your ideal customer and know him intimately. You focused on how you're different from each of your competitors. You expressed the reputation or image you want people to have of your company, through the brand attributes you selected.

Now what the heck do you do with it? This is where it all comes together, so hold onto your hat.

I have to be honest. Branding is a blend of art, science, and inspiration. Collecting data is important for our final conclusions, but most of the time, the magic happens during the questioning process itself, when clients talk through things. Images begin to emerge, patterns form, certain words come up over and over again. I can start to see when people authentically "light up" as they discuss their business or customers, versus when they're just paying lip service to something because they think they should. I take note of all of this during the process and probe further until we get to the core, whether we're talking about brand attributes, benefits, or fleshing out the ideal customer. In this way, you could say branding is part psychology as well. And that would make sense, given branding is all about persuasion, perception, and visceral emotion.

As much as I can, I'm going to show you how to use certain answers to snap together the important pieces. But I'd be lying if I said the process is purely academic. Research plays an important role in informing the brand elements, but pay attention to the process itself so you can see the real insights when they appear.

Remember our graphic from Part 1 showing Brand Strategy as the foundation for the rest of your marketing activities?

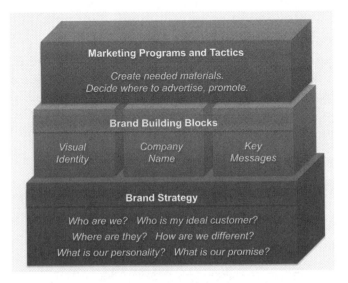

We saw it made practical sense to answer these ten questions before creating your Brand Building Blocks, as now you have an idea of what you want them to communicate to the world. We also saw how your Brand Strategy forms the basis of your marketing plan, and that Building Blocks can be mixed and matched to provide the content for the tactics you have chosen. Your Brand Building Blocks consist of...

- Company name
- Visual identity system: Logo, colors and style guide
- Key Messages Document, which consists of your mission, vision, tagline, company descriptors, brand positioning statement, executive biographies and a press release boilerplate

With these items in hand, you can now mix and match them for any marketing plan you create. Your standard documentation can be used by all your employees, as well as contractors, designers, or writers to help them hit the ground running. This will help you communicate the brand consistently across all touch points and channels.

Brand Building Blocks: Choosing a Name

Now that you know who you are, what you offer, to whom you offer it, and what type of personality you want your organization to have, you're ready to choose a powerful name – whether for your company as a whole or a new product. Naming can be a tricky business, but there are some guidelines you can follow.

First, look at the business description from Question One, and then consider the brand attributes. Knowing what you offer and how you want to be perceived can help you find the right tone for your name. If everything about your business screams formal and conservative, a name like Yahoo or Bing may not work for you.

Next, consider your ideal audience. To whom does the name need to appeal? A company appealing to 70-year old retirees in a small Midwestern town might need a different name than one appealing to 25-year old graphic designers in L.A. Your name should resonate for the audience, so perhaps you can use analogies or references that are age or interest appropriate to help them make sense of you.

Factor in your benefit statements and your greatest asset. Is there a name that conveys any of these? For example, if you're a spa and your benefits are serenity and relaxation and your one greatest asset is that you have the most comfortable massage tables known to man, you may want to find a name that signifies comfort, rest, and tranquility. Another spa owner with a vivacious personality might emphasize how her services provide energy and vigor, so she picks a name evoking more spark and action. If certain names are overused, perhaps your brand lends itself to names or phrases in another language. Maybe our first spa could choose an Italian or French word that means comfort or serenity.

This is where the art comes in. People get paid a lot of money to come up with names, because it can be hard to pick just the right one. In addition, made-up names that actually work aren't that easy to create. Just look at the mess tech and Internet companies made with names that were just wacky and unpronounceable. I mean, really: Xoopit, Eskobo, Renkoo, Otavo, Oyogi or Qoop? And before you lynch me, "Google" is actually derived from a real word, "googol" which means ten to the hundredth power and aligns with the company's original promise of finding any piece of information within the seemingly endless Internet labyrinth.

I have faith that by doing the Brand Strategy steps, your creative juices will flow and you'll find words or phrases that will resonate with you and your customers. You need to like the name yourself. After all, it's your business!

I've often come up with names while answering the ten questions. Certain words start bubbling up to the surface. If you're stuck, get some close business partners or ideal customers together and run an informal focus group where you can brainstorm names. If you do this exercise with friends or family, I highly suggest getting business feedback on the names you come up with from ideal customers or business partners who may have a more objective point of view. What sounds great to your single 27 year-old brother-in-law, may tank with your ideal customer, a 45-year old mother of two.

Be careful to choose just a few of the right people to get input from so you don't end up choosing a "name by committee."

You'll end up running in circles and never make a decision with too much input.

One of my favorite brainstorming tricks is using Thesaurus. com for inspiration. Type in the brand attributes or benefits you've chosen and see what pops up. You never know which words will hit just the right chord to inspire you.

Take a look at the competitors you listed out in your Brand Strategy. Can you come up with a name that will stand out from that crowd? Do you see a theme emerging from their names that you can break away from? For example, many accountants, financial services companies or jewelers carry a family name or the founder's name. This could be because trust and familiarity are the most important attribute for their target audience. If you want to stand out, however, consider picking a name that's more emotional or attribute-focused.

Marty Neumeier, author of *The Brand Gap* and *Zag* (New Riders Press) and an award-winning brand strategist, offers seven criteria for picking a good name:[11]

1. Distinctiveness : Does it stand out, especially from the competition? Does it separate well from ordinary text and speech, meaning does it avoid sounding too generic? He says the best brand names have the "presence" of a proper noun.

2. Brevity: Is it short enough to be easily recalled and used? Can it be shortened to a meaningless acronym or nickname? If so, avoid it.

---

[11] Criteria listed with author permission from *The Brand Gap (New Riders Press)*

3.   Appropriateness: Is there a reasonable fit for the business purpose? If it would work just as well – or better – for another entity, keep looking.

4.   Easy Spelling and Pronunciation: Will most people be able to spell the word after hearing it? Will they be able to pronounce it? As Marty states, a name shouldn't turn into a spelling test or make people feel stupid.

5.   Likability: Will people enjoy using it? Is it intellectually stimulating or does it have a good "mouth feel"? Just ask how much I loved running around the house shouting, "Bing!" after Microsoft introduced their decision engine.

6.   Extendability: Does the name have "legs?" Can it be visually interpreted or lend itself to a number of creative executions? Great names provide endless opportunities for word play, Marty says. With my own firm, Red Slice, I have visual imagery of a red apple standing apart in a sea of green apples and I carry over the fruit analogy with phrases like "take a bite," "fresh and juicy branding" and "crisp messaging." My newsletter is called "Brand Bites" and my basic branding package is called a Brand Juicer. There are endless ways I can play with this brand and the name and they all get back to my core attributes of fresh, smart, and sassy.

7.   Protectability: Can it be trademarked? This is the "science" part of the equation. Can you get a good URL for your website that makes sense and won't confuse people? Some names are more defensible than others, making them safer and more valuable in the long run.

Marty says that high-imagery names are usually more memorable than low-imagery names. Many Greek or Latin root words are low imagery, because they don't help people form a mental picture (Accenture, Innoveda). But names like Apple or Betty Crocker create vivid mental images for people – and combine well with a visual treatment to create a memorable brand icon. One small business, Unicycle Creative, found exactly the right name that not only conveyed their business mission, but also created opportunities for wordplay and brand extension, as you will see from their Brand at Work case study that follows.

BRAND AT WORK: UNICYCLE CREATIVE

A name built upon a strong Brand Strategy can provide countless brand extension ideas. Take Lorne Craig, President and Owner of Unicycle Creative (www.unicyclecreative. com), a Vancouver-based marketing consultancy. The company mission is to help sustainability-focused companies move forward with superior marketing strategy, branding, and communications. A sustainability-focused company may be producing a traditional product or service that uses fewer resources or creates less waste, giving them a product or service niche to improve ecological or social conditions.

Curious, sustainable, quirky, unique, and simple are the brand attributes Lorne wanted to communicate – and he found the perfect metaphor in "Unicycle Creative."

First of all, he showcased the fact that he's a one-person shop with partnerships and subcontractors. Second, the unicycle is quirky and attracts curiosity, much as the company name does – and Lorne himself sometimes rides one to meetings. Third, the unicycle metaphor provides opportunities for wordplay and brand analogies for his messaging.

"We ride economic cycles and business cycles while we recycle and ponder the carbon cycle," Lorne explains, "but there really is just one cycle. One ride. On a unicycle, there is no coasting. One is always in motion, always balancing, yet leaving only the smallest track upon the planet. Unicycle Creative is an efficient and streamlined agency, owned and operated by a single individual working with a network of partner businesses."

The brand further influences Lorne's client selection and business practices. "We have turned down work in the past because the companies in question had not, in our opinion, done enough to improve their environmental or social impact," Lorne says. He also tries to partner and support other sustainable businesses in his work: printers who use eco-friendly inks or suppliers who use recycled materials. And his own business cards were created from items found in his recycle bin, garnering him national recognition from Applied Arts Magazine. Lorne also relies heavily on his blog, (www.greenbriefs.ca), as his main marketing vehicle, allowing him to comment on green marketing issues, generate feedback, and approach new clients without sending a single sheet of paper.

Brand Building Blocks: Creating your Visual Identity System

Now that you have your Brand Strategy all thought out and you know who you're trying to reach with what messages, you're ready to design a logo and other visual identity pieces. Even though nine times out ten, businesses start with the logo and work backwards, if you're a new business, I implore you to do things in the right order. The clients I talk to who didn't work this way often spent thousands of dollars on designers who just "didn't get it." One client went through four different designers and thousands of dollars trying to get her logo just right. It might not be the designer's fault: as we saw earlier, a designer's job is to take a concept or message and communicate it visually. If he received no guidance on what that message was, or to whom it was speaking, then he was grasping at straws.

Don't underestimate the power of a logo.

Hopefully you'll be living with it for awhile and will spend money on marketing, production, and customer service to make that logo *mean something* to your audience. Aren't you asking that logo to do part of the heavy lifting for you and communicate something before you even say a word?

I know, I know. A logo is just a graphic, a picture. How can you communicate everything about a business and what you provide in one little thing? The truth is, you can't communicate *everything*, but you can communicate *something*.

Even though taste is subjective, aesthetics do matter subconsciously to human perceptions. I once asked a creative director, "But what difference does it really make? If the client wants to tweak something this way or that, shouldn't we be okay with that?"

He sighed and said, "Yes, Maria, but there are fundamental truths to good design, balance, placement, and typography that the human eye will absorb and base opinions on. And the client can't fight that. It's our job to create a logo or ad that stays true to human design principles as a whole and carefully balances that with personal preferences – otherwise what are they paying us for?"

This is true of logos, colors, shapes, typefaces, placement, and size – all of these make an impression and mean something to a customer. While it's true that a logo I think is cheesy might seem elegant to someone else, a great designer knows where universal human truths come into play. Many business owners create logos on the cheap, resulting in poor color choices, even worse font choices, and placement that's either too busy and jarring, or sparse and unbalanced. After all the logos I've seen and studied, I can spot the poor spacing decisions, logos that give me a headache because there's no focal point, or the ones that won't translate well to other media. And I'm not even a skilled designer.

When designing your logo, you want to factor in your business description, your benefits, brand attributes, and your ideal customer. You can use colors to convey mood and status. Are you a retro company and want to evoke themes from the past? Then you might pick colors from the 70s or 80s. Are you soft and serene? Then pastel or lighter hues may win out over bright, garish shades.

One logo and color palette mistake some companies make is to assume that since they're marketing to women, they need to incorporate pink. Depending on the type of woman (remember, your detailed ideal customer profile), she may be sick of that color or think you're pandering to her. Urban working women may be attracted to a broad range of modern colors you'd find in magazines like *Dwell*. We learned from Bridget Perez of Tray Creative (www.traycreative.com) in Part 1 how color influences the buying decision. Her design work involves finding the right logo and color palette to communicate what you do and why you are different. Bridget says color can evoke strong emotional responses and trigger memories for people. Colors also have specific meaning. For example, green signifies "go," money, or nature, while red signifies "stop," heat, or love. Some meanings are universal, while others are cultural. Sometimes gender also plays a role in color perception.

When it comes to color, the bottom line is to be mindful of why you're selecting it and what it will communicate. Don't just pick your favorite colors.

Think about your audience – the people with whom you're trying to connect. What colors will resonate with them and evoke the appropriate emotional responses about your business? Also consider the industry you're in and who you want to be within the industry. What colors do your competitors use? Is it more strategic to blend in with them, or stand out? In what way can color make your business distinctive? Will the colors you choose translate well and consistently across different media? Are they too trendy and will they become dated? Do they unintentionally evoke negative connotations? With a little research on the meaning of color, your customers, and your competitors, you'll be able to make a well-informed decision about the colors for your company.

The second important factor is font, or typeface. I see many businesses who say they want to be elegant, high-end, and refined, but the company name on their logo is written in a clunky and heavy font – nothing refined or elegant about it. Others want to appeal to a modern sensibility, but use a traditional, old-fashioned Serif font.

Ayesha Mathews-Wadhwa, Chief Pixel Bender for PixInk Design (www.pixinkdesign.com) says that font adds the sparkle to a logo or company identity. "It's crucial for brands to pick a font not simply for its popularity, but for the right message it communicates about the brand," she says. "This enhances the features of the brand visually."

Is your brand timeless, vintage, and classic? A script or serif font (the fonts with little "tags" on the ends of each letter, such as you see in Times New Roman) may be appropriate. Serif fonts have been around for centuries and denote dependability.

Ayesha says you also need to consider where this font will be seen. While some fonts may work for a logo, you might want to be careful using certain fonts for your website copy. "The serifs could clutter a paragraph on the web, but shouldn't be avoided in logos or other main design elements," Ayesha cautions.

Sans Serifs are used for a modern, clean, sleek look. They reek of efficiency, simplicity and innovation. The opposite of serif fonts, these look great on a small screen.

Think about your brand attributes when picking the font for both your logo and your copy. Is your company loud, energetic, fun, and imaginative? Maybe you should consider a decorative font. These are great for brands geared towards entertainment and children. Is your brand strong, confident, and manly? Pick fonts with square, right angles. Bold and other heavily structured fonts clearly communicate this message. A transportation company, financial institution, durable products distributor, or law office might consider these. Is the brand feminine, graceful, beautiful, and delicate? Script fonts are a good solution.

"Fonts carry the most important first impressions to the customer in the form of collateral, letterhead, web pages, promotional items, advertisements, business cards, brochures and package designs," says Ayesha. "They can stimulate opinions about company character, moral aptitude, and credibility. It is vital to get the right help for this responsibility."

Brand Building Blocks: Crafting Your Key Messages

Now that you have your Brand Strategy baked, you're ready to build your key corporate messages. You can put these together into a Key Messages Document and refer to it over and over again. Not only will this save you time when asked for information, but you'll maintain consistency in all places where people see you and your brand. In addition, you get the added benefit of having a cheat sheet for employees to ensure their messages are consistent and clear. The last thing you want is people making up their own versions of your company description or tagline on the fly.

The Key Messages Document I use with my clients consists of the following parts:

- Brand positioning statement
- Mission
- Vision
- Tagline
- 25-, 50-, and 100-word company descriptors
- Benefits
- Differentiators
- Executive bios
- Press release boilerplate
- Elevator pitch

Brand Positioning Statement

The brand positioning statement is a paragraph that encapsulates the entire Brand Strategy process and all your answers. Most of the time, you'll be able to send all ten of these questions and answers to a designer or writer as background info. But sometimes, you want to sum it all up in an explanatory paragraph for your designer or writer – or even for yourself.

You may also include it in orientation materials to ensure your employees understand what you're all about. This is where you can use those analogies to other brands, characters, and famous people you thought through in your Brand Attributes answer.

This statement is for internal or agency use only – not meant to be customer-facing. Later on, you'll develop "customer-ready" copy that is informed by this statement. It's just a way of showing what you want your business to be and how you'd like it to be perceived.

Here's a brand positioning statement example from a massage and bodywork client:

> 66 Alinga Bodywork is the Anthropologie of the bodywork field, offering a unique, creative, individual approach to bodywork (massage, Reiki and BodyTalk) combined with attentive and personalized service that is in tune with the way you express yourself and your personal truth. It provides high value, yet affordable services to busy women that go beyond just surface pampering to something deeper and more lasting. Unlike pure massage therapists, Andrea uses the body as an access point to specifically identify what is holding you back by releasing physical tension and unprocessed emotions. This release helps you get unstuck creatively and emotionally. Sessions at Alinga provide a lasting investment in your self-development that goes beyond pure pampering.
>
> Alinga is focused on balance, action, forward movement, and progress. It propels clients to the next level by shifting them out of stagnation and into action, in their lives or work, using a body-centered approach to process the physical and emotional/energetic issues holding them

back. It opens them up to new possibilities, giving them the clarity and the confidence to manifest a new reality, whether that be launching or expanding a business, jumping feet first into exploring art, music, or higher education, or creating space in daily life to be more present in the moment and connected to the body.**"**

This brand positioning statement was a carefully worded summary of the ten answers. The business owner created this summary after putting time and thought into her audience, brand attributes, differentiators, and customer benefits. She incorporated analogies to better-known brands to bring certain images and feelings to mind. We know which slot she wants to occupy in someone's brain. Certain words and phrases came up over and over during the process and we paid attention to those in building her brand positioning, as well as her tagline and mission statement.

Mission and Vision

The mission and vision also become clear at you move through the ten question Brand Strategy process. As you think about your company's reason for being, your goals, the image you want to project, and the people you serve, you begin expanding your definition of what you want your company to be. I find just talking to a business owner and asking, "Why did you start this business?" can yield the seeds of a mission or vision statement. They use certain words or phrases over and over again. As you think through the Brand Strategy, certain themes that consistently emerge will be strong clues to your mission and vision.

The mission and vision not only help you keep the end in mind at all times, they will also inspire your customers –and your employees.

Yes, we know your primary goal is to make money, but customers and employees want to connect with your business on a deeper level. They want to know their buying choices and work efforts are relevant to a higher goal. This motivates people and helps them form loyal connections.

Mission

Your mission statement is a precise definition of what your organization does on a daily basis and what you want to accomplish. It should describe the business you're in and provide a definition of why the organization exists. Try and keep this to one or two sentences in length. Some example mission statements:

- Make flying good again" (Virgin America)
- "Our mission: to inspire and nurture the human spirit – one person, one cup, and one neighborhood at a time." (Starbucks)
- "The mission of Southwest Airlines is dedication to the highest quality of Customer Service delivered with a sense of warmth, friendliness, individual pride, and Company Spirit." (Southwest Airlines)
- "To provide effective means for the prevention of cruelty to animals throughout the United States" (ASPCA)
- "Women for Women International provides women survivors of war, civil strife and other conflicts with the tools and resources to move from crisis and poverty to stability and self-sufficiency, thereby promoting viable civil societies. We're changing the world one woman at a time" (Women for Women International)

As a personal bias, I think mission statements like, "To provide the best customer service and product quality" are too generic. Try and put your mission statement in the context of what you do, while still leaving room to expand your offerings. The mission at Red Slice, my firm, is "To engage, inform, and delight your target audience." This has to do with providing marketing and branding strategies that get attention (engage), let audiences know a bit more about the company and why they're different (inform), and provide a connection (delight.) Incidentally, this is my personal mission in all my writing and workshop pursuits as well, so it applies broadly to other services the business offers and leaves room for growth.

Small businesses can create a mission statement so inspiring they may not require a vision statement. But if you have a loftier goal in mind for the future of your company, then a vision statement is a great way to frame that.

Vision

Rebecca Rodskog of Rodskog Change Consulting (www. rodskog.com) helps businesses and individuals get from Point A to Point B. As an experienced change management consultant and personal development professional, Rebecca is often tasked with crafting vision and mission statements for complex projects, so companies don't lose sight of the end goal. She also creates mission and vision statements for individuals. Rebecca advises clients who are creating a vision statement to ask themselves: "What is our ideal preferred future?" and be sure to...

- Draw on the beliefs, mission, and environment of the organization,
- Describe what you want to see in the future,
- Be positive and inspiring,
- Don't assume the system will have the same framework as it does today,
- Be open to dramatic modifications to current organization, methodology, teaching techniques, facilities, etc.

Ask yourself:
- Where will my company be in the long term?
- Will it be the premier provider of a particular product or service? Will it be in the top ten international players in a particular market?
- What is the ultimate "to-be" state for my company?

You may not require an actual vision "statement", as long as you can paint a clear, compelling picture that drives the business forward. These could be ideals or lofty goals that rally the internal troops and help customers connect with you. Below you'll find sample vision statements from several companies. You'll note these contain ambitious visions that go beyond day-to-day operations and the specific market spaces in which these organizations play today. They paint a picture of an ideal future if the business does well.

~ ~ ~ ~

Women for Women International envisions a world where no one is abused, poor, illiterate, or marginalized; where members of communities have full and equal participation in the processes that ensure their health, well-being and economic independence, and where everyone has the freedom to define the scope of their life, their future, and strive to achieve their full potential. (Women for Women International)

~ ~ ~ ~

I believe that this nation should commit itself to achieving the goal, before this decade is out, of landing a man on the Moon and returning him safely to the Earth. (President John F. Kennedy, 1961)

~ ~ ~ ~

Coca Cola's vision statement is actually a multi-part credo:

People: Be a great place to work where people are inspired to be the best they can be.

Portfolio: Bring to the world a portfolio of quality beverage brands that anticipate and satisfy people's desires and needs.

Partners: Nurture a winning network of customers and suppliers, together we create mutual, enduring value.

Planet: Be a responsible citizen that makes a difference by helping build and support sustainable communities.

Profit: Maximize long-term return to shareowners while being mindful of our overall responsibilities.

Productivity: Be a highly effective, lean and fast-moving organization.

In summary, your mission is what drives you on a day-to-day basis. It's the reason your product or service is in existence, and it defines the "why" behind the thing you're creating.

Your vision is the end state: what you ultimately want your company to become and the impact you want to have on your customers and the world. Your mission and vision create the framework and inspiration your organization and its employees need to be successful. An old Japanese proverb eloquently states the important symbiotic relationship between vision and action: *Vision without action is a daydream. Action without vision is a nightmare.*

Tagline

The tagline is another element that almost always falls out of the Brand Strategy process. It's a short, punchy, memorable phrase that can be used in advertising and on company materials. The tagline sums up what you're all about in a memorable way, either in actual words or the tone of those words. A tagline could accompany your logo at all times, and in fact be part of it. Or you can have a tagline you only use on certain materials, not officially integrated with your logo. The choice is yours.

As you talk through your vision, goals, and benefits, certain words and sayings will keep bubbling to the surface. Jot down the little inspirations that pop up during the process, even if they don't apply to the question you're answering. This is exactly how I've stumbled upon great taglines for my clients.

> You want a tagline to be short and sweet, not a long, descriptive sentence. You want something people will remember.

Alliterations often work well, or several short words or phrases. Here are some examples:

Pampering with Purpose (for a massage and bodywork business)

Informed Girls. Empowered Women (for a company providing advice for parents of young girls who are going through puberty)

Branch Out. Live Richly! (for a career consultant who helps people with multiple passions define financially and emotionally rewarding careers that encompass them all.)

Grow. (for a consultant and life coach who helps individuals and organizations deal with and adapt to change in an opportunistic way)

You want to avoid a boring, descriptive sentence as a tagline, such as, "Helping women build and create their own businesses." While that may indeed be the organization's mission statement, it isn't memorable (or short) enough to use in advertising or with a logo. Instead, take inspiration from Hatch Network (www. hatchnetwork.com), a women's entrepreneurial community based in San Francisco. Hatch Network is a community of contributors who all have the same goal: to become wise and successful entrepreneurs with businesses that are sustainable in a changing economy. Members contribute time, energy, and experience to one another and, in return, benefit from the insightful stories and enthusiastic support. Founders Allison Covarrubias and Claire Fontana describe their venture as "a modern business school where women start and grow their business together." That one-liner echoes their company description. But their actual tagline is more catchy and fun: *Learn, Lead, and Support.*

Here are other examples of memorable taglines:

"The ultimate driving machine"

"Just do it"

"Made from the best stuff on Earth"

"You're in good hands"

"Fly the friendly skies"

"Does a body good"

One last thing to note is the difference between taglines and campaign slogans. *Taglines* are all-encompassing and represent the company at a macro level. They last for awhile, until perhaps the company rebrands. A *slogan* is a theme used in a specific multi-channel ad campaign, and when the campaign ends, the campaign "tagline" (slogan) goes away. Examples of this would be Southwest Airlines "Grab your bags. It's on" recent ad campaign; Bud Light's "The difference is drinkability"; or Coca Cola's "Open Happiness". These are not corporate taglines per se, but specific campaign slogans that are temporal in nature. If you have limited budget and time, it might be best to find one permanent tagline to hang your hat on and get in front of customers for a longer period of time, rather than confuse them with different slogans.

Company Descriptors

Standard company descriptors will be a useful tool for your business. Inevitably, you'll need to provide someone with a short description of your firm: for a trade show program, an ad link on a partner site, or when you sponsor a direct mail piece. You're often bound by space and character constraints, so it's helpful to prepare 25-word, 50-word, and 100-word descriptors in advance. This also helps when others within the organization need to send a description out as part of a proposal or brochure.

Many folks use this verbiage on the About page of their website. Again, you should create this in advance, because you don't want everyone coming up with their own definitions and inventing messages on the fly.

To create this information, use elements of the company description you created in Question One, combined with a few benefits you provide and something about the audience you serve. You also may want to list your website address in the description, so people can go there for more information. Here's an example from a client:

> CareerBranches is the premier boutique career design agency for multi-talented individuals who simply can't pick just one career. CareerBranches's coaching and career design services help modern-day "Renaissance Personalities" claim their place in today's specialist society and thrive in their careers and lives. Explore the possibilities at www. careerbranches.com.

The description takes into account what she does (coaching and career design services), for whom she does it (people who have multiple talents and have trouble choosing just one career path), and gives her URL for more information. If she ever sponsors an event or has a partner link next to her logo on another site, she can use this same description everywhere to ensure consistency and clarity.

Here's another example, from an eCommerce client:

> Dot Girl Products offers products and resources that help parents comfortably talk to and reassure their young daughters about womanhood. Our signature product, The Dot Girls First Period Kit, is a stylish and discreet carrying case with all the essentials a girl needs for her first period, including pads, calendar, scented wipes, heating pad, and a Guide to Menstruation. The Guide answers all of the questions a young girl may have and helps parents easily and lovingly start the conversation. Our vision is to create empowered, informed, and happy young women who take a positive first step into womanhood.

This descriptor incorporated the vision of helping create healthy, empowered young women as a result of their work. It also describes the product they sell and who they serve (parents of young girls).

> With this standard descriptor, the company is secure in the fact that any employee or partner can provide a consistent descriptor for materials or sponsorship.

When working for tech companies in the past, I was always ready when a trade show organizer asked for a one-line descriptor for their website or when a partner asked for a few lines to accompany our logo on their website. I recommend you start by building the long one (100 words or less) first, so you can include everything you want, and then editing down to the most crucial points, rather than starting with the shortest one and building up.

Benefits and Differentiators

Your Key Messages document should list the main corporate benefits and core differentiators you want to tout in all of your messaging. You came up with this list in the Brand Strategy process, and placing it in the Key Messages Document captures everything in one place for easy reference. Some small businesses can get away with a simple bulleted list of benefits and differentiators, but others, especially technology companies, expand on this concept and create a *messaging platform*. This matrix is used as an outline for all other written communications: sales presentations, website copy, brochures, etc. It contains...

- The company's overall, high-level value proposition,
- Three main benefits the company offers,
- Three main capabilities that support each benefit claim (how do you provide that benefit?),
- Three main proof points or features that support each capability (what proof do you have that you can do what you say you can do? Why are you able to offer that capability?).

Some businesses do this process in reverse, especially product or technology companies. They first look at all their product features and group them under certain functions or capabilities. Then they group and roll up those capabilities under certain benefit headings. For example, you could look at features of a car: Early accident warning system, side-impact airbags, and ergonomic safety belts. With these features, the carmaker can state that it provides state-of-the-art automotive safety technology. That capability in turn offers the end benefit of "keeping your family safe" to customers.

Listing your benefits and differentiators will ensure your employees as well as hired writers and designers are clear on what your business offers to customers and what you feel is most important. Your advertising copy will consistently reflect the right points. When customers who see your messages in multiple places and on multiple occasions see and hear the same thing, the message is more likely to stick in their minds. Your messaging platform can later be condensed to craft the Elevator Pitch, which we'll talk about in a moment.

A bulleted list of your differentiators can quickly bring someone up to speed on the main ways you're better than your competition. The list will make ad development and copy writing easier, and is another way to practice clarity and consistency in everything you do. Rather than let a writer, an employee, or even a partner decide their own interpretation, you create a master list from which everyone works to ensure all communication vehicles emphasize the right points.

Executive Biographies

The executive biography, or bio, is exactly that: A short, one-paragraph biography for each key executive that you can use on the website or for introductions at speaking engagements. I include biographies in the Key Messages document because they're an important part of your communications – and, more importantly, because you may want to emphasize certain experiences or details in the executive's background that will back up your Brand Strategy.

Many organizations ignore this as a communication vehicle and whip up a boilerplate bio rather than use it as another simple yet effective branding opportunity.

All of your corporate messaging pieces should work together to support the brand, and bios are no exception. For example, if your brand is playful and casual, you won't write a stiff, boring bio for your website. You may want to talk about favorite trips the executives have taken or activities they enjoy.

If your brand is devoted to community philanthropy, you'll want to highlight the volunteer organizations to which the key executives donate their time and talents. Should your brand emphasize family, home, and work-life balance, you'll mention the hobbies or family interests of each executive. If you sell athletic apparel and accessories, maybe you want to mention each executives' favorite sport. The point is that a bio is yet another vital customer touch point to help solidify your organization's image and verbally communicate your brand promise.

You can use your bio to jazz things up and differentiate yourself. Starting your bio with what you're passionate about or your personal mission can be far more interesting and engaging than a bland resumé regurgitation. Every communication with your audience can help build up the brand you want in their minds, and a bio is no exception.

Press Boilerplate

Your press release boilerplate is the final standard tool you'll need in your messaging bag of tricks. As you write press releases to promote your business, you need to include standard boilerplate language at the end of each one. You often see these in the form of "About" sections at the end of the release. This gives the media background on your company, so you don't have to spend a paragraph talking about it in the release itself and can jump right to the meat of the news story. The press release boilerplate is often derived from the company descriptor, with a few other facts thrown in, such as the year you were founded, location, and perhaps number of stores. The release often lists a general sales contact phone number or website address. Here's an example:

66 Dot Girl First Period Products offers products and resources that help parents comfortably talk to and reassure their young daughters about menstruation. Founded by sisters Terri Goodwin and Kathy Pickus, the company helps ease parents into an often difficult conversation and creates empowered young women who have a positive first period experience.

Their signature product, The Dot Girls First Period Kit™, is a stylish and discreet carrying case with all the essentials a girl needs for her first period, including a pad, calendar, scented wipes, heating pad and a Guide to Menstruation. The Guide answers all of the questions a young girl may have and helps mothers easily and lovingly start the conversation. The company was founded in 2006 and is based in Seattle, Washington. Visit us at (www.dotgirlproducts.com). 99

Crafting a Killer Elevator Pitch

I'm often amazed at how many clients come to me for help on the elevator pitch before they've done due diligence on their Brand Strategy. You'll have difficulty knowing what needs to be communicated in an elevator pitch if you don't yet have a good sense of your benefits, differentiators, and ideal customers.

Many a Silicon Valley start-up was funded via a catchy elevator pitch. But this simple marketing tool does more than help you get investors. You'll use this handy tool anytime you speak in public about your business. I've seen many small business owners stumble when introducing themselves at a networking event or panel discussion because they don't have their elevator pitch truly baked. Sometimes they even leave the audience wondering if they provide a product or a service, the most fundamental point about what they do.

An elevator pitch is so named because if you were on an elevator with someone who asked about your organization, you'd only have so many floors to give a clear answer.

> An elevator pitch is your 30-second to one-minute long response to the question, "What does your company do?"

The pitch requires you to go one step deeper on your claims, citing examples and proof points of how or why you do this. It's the story you tell to intrigue listeners, giving them a desire to learn more about your firm and what you do. The best framework for creating your elevator pitch is to combine the answers about your company description, your benefits and your differentiators into one short, smooth and flowing story.

- Start with an overall proposition sentence – best to make this mission-driven, (i.e., Yoga Yoga offers yoga and meditation classes that help clients connect to their center and balance their lives).

- Cite three main benefits you offer. If you have a list of ten, then pick the three most important things you want people to remember. The more information you throw at people, the less anything will stick, so carefully choose only three main points. The idea is to pique their interest, not tell them everything in 30 seconds. *We increase energy, reduce stress, and improve your body's flexibility.*

- Cite a capability that illustrates how you deliver each benefit. This is the "And what I mean by that is...." description of your benefit point. For example, for "reduce stress" our owner might say: *Our yoga classes give you a quiet space to meditate and breathe, and the practice can help you take a break from your hectic life.*

- Cite a proof point for each capability – tell me why only you can make this claim. *Our clients report healthy or lowered blood pressures as a result of working with us.*

- End with a one-sentence summary. This could even be your tagline. *Yoga Yoga connects your body and mind so you can live in great harmony.*

You may not have time to say all of this in every instance, but you can scale the model to fit the allotted time. For example, if you only have 15 seconds, give your opening line, three main benefits, and your closing summary.

An elevator pitch is meant to be spoken, so use words you are comfortable actually saying and yet still convey passion and excitement.

Elevator pitches are important when you network, speak in public, and just generally tell people about your business.

The summary or closing line is especially important to nail down, because you don't want to commit the biggest networking sin: ending your pitch with, "Okay, so, um, yeah, that's it. That's what we do." As a track coach of mine once said, "You need to finish strong!" You want to leave a confident impression in people's minds, which is why I suggest ending with a tagline. And, since your employees represent you, you need to be sure they know the pitch as well. They can make the words their own over time, so they don't all sound like robots, but you can rest assured that no matter which employee a customer meets, they'll get a consistent business description.

At many software companies for which I worked, we gathered feedback from employees before crafting the pitch, to see what resonated for them. This gave us their buy-in. Then we asked every salesperson to memorize it and even quizzed them on it at sales meetings.

Use Brand to Guide Your Marketing Investments

Now that you have a Brand Strategy mapped out and you've crafted a visual identity and messaging, you're prepared to make smart investment decisions. Remember when we created the ideal customer profile in rich detail? Now you can decide which marketing vehicles will get you in front of the right customers – and which ones will be a total waste of time.

Review your ideal customer profile and that person's "day in the life." Are they watching TV or do they mostly get information from the Web? Do they listen to the radio or read magazines? What organizations and clubs do they belong to? As you review this information you'll start to see interesting marketing opportunities to guide your decisions.

This is where you decide if social media is the right tactic for you – and if so, what social media channels to use. For example, businesses that target Internet-savvy brides-to-be might be interested to know that as of February 2010 nearly two million female Facebook users are proudly sporting the "engaged" relationship status. If your business targets those ladies, you can reach them using Facebook's targeted advertising platform. Hazel Grace Dircksen, founder of Socialbees (www.socialbeesstrategy.com), a Facebook consultancy, often helps clients narrow their searches with micro-targeting options based on their target audience. Facebook uses profile demographics and keywords that allow advertisers to reach even more specific users, such as eco-brides, fashion conscious brides, athletic brides, etc.

Until you know your own audience intimately, any demographic data that an ad sales rep puts in front of you will be useless because you won't know if that's who you want to reach. When placing an ad or buying a booth at an event, you need to ask the sales rep for an audience profile or demographic data. Even better, do they have psychographic data profiling the wants, needs, and behaviors of the audience? Then you can decide if that vehicle fits your ideal customer. Don't be lulled by promises of "quantity" when it's "quality" you're after. For example, suppose a large conference attracts 5,000 moms and asks your mom-focused business to sponsor a booth. But what if those moms are in a lower-income bracket and have no disposable income to spend on your luxury high-end product? Or your product is for toddler moms, but the show only attracts moms of college students? This is an extreme example, but nine times out of ten, small business owners *assume* something will be a good marketing opportunity based on quantity, so they don't ask the right questions to dig deeper. They also don't factor in whether the brand of the event, magazine, or website is a good fit with their own brand. This is because they haven't defined their own brand clearly enough.

Now that you have a Brand Strategy, you can better decide which places align well with your brand and which could damage it. For example, a high-end luxury jeweler may not choose to spend their limited marketing budget on *The National Enquirer* or sponsoring a Pay-Per-View wrestling match, no matter how great the advertising deal sounds. They want to advertise and partner with vehicles that hit the same ideal customer and have a similar brand caliber that won't damage brand equity.

Choosing the right marketing vehicles is one of the most important ways to ensure your brand is consistently represented.

The Brand at Work case study on CRAVE that follows shows how a well-crafted ideal customer profile and Brand Strategy can save you money and effort by helping you avoid tactics that are not a good fit for your business.

〰〰〰〰〰〰〰〰〰〰〰〰〰〰〰〰〰〰〰〰〰〰〰〰〰〰〰〰

BRAND AT WORK: CRAVE

Serial entrepreneur Melody Biringer has a firm vision of her ideal customer, and that has made all the difference to the success of The CRAVE company (www.thecravecompany. com). CRAVE is an innovative women's media company that connects urban gals in specific cities to the sassiest, gutsiest, most inspiring people they need to know in town through parties, gatherings, and online networking. What initially started in 2001 as a way for Melody to spend more time relaxing, indulging, shopping, and styling with her girlfriends has turned into a multi-city international venture. The secret is that the CRAVE brand has local presence in each of its markets, such as CRAVEseattle and CRAVEamsterdam, so it creates personal local connections.

Melody targets two distinct audiences: female consumers and female business owners. On one side, her parties and events attract the urban-minded woman in her 30s or 40s who's an independent thinker and fashion lover. She's healthy, stylish, connected, and the go-to woman in her circle of friends. On the other hand, Melody's business networking component includes workshops, conferences, and city guides to help women entrepreneurs grow their businesses and attract new customers. The profile for the ideal CRAVE business owner is a woman in her 40s, doing her own thing and following her passion – be it jewelry making, building websites, or expanding a local boutique chain. For her, lifestyle is more important than money, and she's wants to control her life and be her own boss.

Both audience groups earn a household income upwards of $75,000 per year. "The CRAVE brand is all about celebrating independent and stylish women who are doing cool things in every city we're in," says Melody. "It's about creating connections and fostering innovation among women. We want to bring women-owned businesses and their desired customers together to learn, connect, and inspire."

Melody's brand combines style, powerful femininity, innovation, and community and guides each of her decisions, including which markets to enter, how to promote her company, and how she selects women-owned businesses for the city guides. "We stick with urban areas where lots of style and inspiration can be found. We also never do broad ads because our brand is all about connections and word of mouth," she says. "CRAVE is the secret that the most stylish and successful women share with their girlfriends. If we did mainstream ads, we would lose that brand essence and we wouldn't attract the independent woman we seek who wants to be the first to discover a unique find."

This strong brand definition means CRAVE stays away from big conferences and events where other women's groups may be. Most of their promotion comes from word of mouth, email marketing, press coverage, and extensive use of social media to get the buzz going.

The Rule of Three

When putting together your marketing plan, it's important to know where your ideal buying audience goes. Try to be in those places. And so you don't lose your sanity trying to promote and advertise everywhere, go deep rather than broad. By this I mean identify a few key publications, websites, or events that are exactly the right fit for you and create an integrated marketing package with each ad sales rep. Most small businesses don't have the budget to do a lot of advertising and marketing in every single place their ideal customer might be. So pick a few partners and try to do as much as you can with each one, versus a one-time shot across many different vehicles.

I call this following the *Rule of Three*. In a given month or quarter, depending on your budget, focus on three publications, three website partners, three events, etc.

> Engaging in fewer activities, but more of the right ones, will be more effective than skipping a stone across the lake and barely making a splash with each marketing vehicle.

For example, you might partner with a website that fits your audience profile and negotiate the following add-ons:

- a dedicated email to their subscriber list,
- exposure at an event or webcast they're sponsoring,
- online ads in different forums over a three- or six-month period, rather than just a one-time ad,
- permission to write an article or blog post on a brand-related topic.

Many ad sales reps are delighted to get creative and you can put a multi-touch or integrated marketing program in place to get your brand and promise in front of the right people multiple times and in multiple ways.

Magazines, radio stations, TV shows, websites, and events all have their own brand promise and attract certain audiences. If you know your brand well, you can confidently decide which ones align with your best possible customers, your values, and your benefits.

The same holds true for deciding on partners. Yes, some distribution partners may give you access to millions of people you'd never be able to reach. But if none of those people will buy from you or be attracted to your brand promise, then that is just money and energy down the drain. You only want to partner with firms that won't downgrade your brand or get you in front of people who won't buy from you. You can see an example of using brand to guide distribution decisions in DRY Soda's Brand at Work case study that follows.

BRAND AT WORK: DRY SODA

A strong Brand Strategy doesn't remain stagnant – it evolves and adapts to changing demands and dynamics, while remaining close to its roots. Sharelle Klaus, Founder and CEO of DRY Soda Company (www.drysoda.com), evolved her strategy while staying true to her mission of creating a new soda category. Sharelle saw a market need for a modern, non-alcoholic beverage when she was pregnant and couldn't drink alcohol.

As a food and wine lover, she grew frustrated with the lack of options available to pair with fine meals. Sharelle hoped for a drink that was simple, all-natural, caffeine-free, low in sugar, and made with the highest quality ingredients – a beverage that would complement great food or act as light refreshment on its own.

DRY Sodas come in seven flavors: cucumber, vanilla bean, juniper berry, lavender, lemongrass, kumquat, and rhubarb. DRYs brand is modern, all-natural, well-designed, and sophisticated. This is conveyed through their gorgeous bottles, their modern and simple visual identity, and the fact that DRY is found only at certain high-end restaurants, stores, and food and wine events.

As the brand grew, they protected it by carefully choosing high-end distribution partners. Initially, they didn't want to mass market it in any way. However, consumer beverage choices are changing and wellness has become a bigger priority to everyone, not just the high-end market. People are cutting down on sugar and First Lady Michelle Obama unveiled an initiative to fight childhood obesity. The New England Journal of Medicine asked soda companies to lower their sweetness level, and DRY Soda was the only one that met the requirement. In keeping with their brand as a "modern soda company," they had to evolve the strategy to meet consumers where they are today. So they increased the flavor choices to include more mainstream preferences, decreased their price point to stay competitive, and opened up more distribution channels. They plan to begin selling through Target – a mass-market brand, but one with a bit more cache and sophistication that aligns well with DRY.

They're staying true to the brand by continuing to choose distribution partners with great care. Partners that don't align with their carefully cultivated brand values will be turned down. As they open up distribution, DRY is finding what "brand levers" work in different markets. But they stay on course to the original brand values of all-natural, sophisticated, modern, and well-designed so as not to alienate their early adopters.

"We still need to build the brand customer-by-customer, even though we're expanding our reach," says Sharelle. "We always want any new consumer's first experience with DRY to be consistent with the brand, and you tell your brand story by where people can find you. We build our brand region by region so people can develop strong emotional attachments, and that approach influences how we roll out the product in each new market." DRY Soda can be found throughout the United States and Canada and in limited international distribution.

Operationalizing Your Brand

So we've seen how brand can inform your visual elements, messaging elements, and marketing tactics. But brand can do even more for your business if you let it. Since brand is grounded in your promise to customers, you need to live your brand in everything you do. This means your company operations as well. Remember, we've talked about brand being conveyed not only visually and verbally but also through experience. Now we'll discuss this "experiential" component. If you're going to talk the talk, you need to walk the walk.

> Brand as a promise and philosophy should influence your organization inside and out: through internal procedures, production processes, partner programs, hiring practices, and even your office and store décor.

Think about a company that promises customer service as their first priority. All their ads communicate personalized service and attention. Their website design and colors are warm and inviting. The tagline even says, "Customers First." Yet when you call their customer service line, you reach a voicemail option from hell that never gets you to a live person and doesn't help answer your question. Worse, when you finally get to an option to "Speak to an operator," you're put on hold with a wait time of 10 minutes while being forced to listen to an automated message claiming, "Your call is important to us." Sound familiar? This is because the brand promise made by the marketing department isn't knitted into the DNA of how the company does business. Somehow the folks in charge of the customer service line weren't included in the branding process to see how their structure, processes – and even the automated technology they may have picked – contributes to the overall brand promise. So the company has an identity crisis. They've told me customers are number one in everything they say, but my experience proves otherwise.

This is what happens when companies think branding is only the marketing department's responsibility. If brand as we've defined it is indeed the sum total of all the customers' experiences, ads they've seen, messages they've heard, even colors or designs that have subconsciously influenced their perception, then...

> Branding is *everyone's* responsibility in the organization.

It starts at the top, but every group from sales, to customer service, to fulfillment, to field operations must understand how the work they do impacts the brand promise. If they can see this, they can begin creating better processes and policies for their own departments that add to the customer experience, in both small and large ways.

For example, if a software business tries to tell me they're trustworthy, stable, and work with high-caliber Fortune 1000 companies, then the accounting department needs to know and own this. Why? Because if I'm a vendor working with that software company and I can't get my invoices paid on time, how will I perceive the company? Vendors within the same industry often work with other companies in that industry, and people talk. Rumors can start flying about your financial viability, the health of your business, and the value of your word. Vendor relations have as important a role to play in branding as do customer experiences. Word gets around, people talk, and pretty soon you'll be dealing with a sullied reputation. I've worked with a few start-up firms who thought it was fine to delay vendor payments by months and months, while promising customers that they were stable and could deliver immediate value. But we all know how small the world can be, and how brand inconsistency across the organization can actually turn customers away. In the following Brand at Work case study, we see how a company needs to walk its talk right from your first exposure to its name, Honest Tea.

BRAND AT WORK: HONEST TEA

With a name like Honest Tea (www.honesttea.com), your brand had better deliver in action as well as message. Founders Barry Nalebuff and Seth Goldman set out to create and promote delicious organic beverages. This mission requires a brand and product that's honest from start to finish, environmentally conscious, and healthy. They live this brand promise by choosing only natural, organic ingredients and supporting Fair Trade farming in the international community.

Honest Tea seeks to create honest relationships with employees, suppliers, customers, and the communities in which they do business, particularly economically disadvantaged communities. They also support small organic farms worldwide. One example is their recent Mate product. Mate leaves produce a similar taste to tea, but offer a smoother taste with different antioxidants. The mate they use comes from an Argentinean family farm whose success shows other farms in the community that organic farming is not only responsible, but profitable.

Honest Tea's environmental stewardship doesn't stop with product decisions. They recently expanded to a new office that was "built green" with re-purposed furniture, reclaimed brick, recycled glass countertops, energy efficient lighting, and bamboo flooring. They also encourage office composting and recycling and provide showers so employees can bike to work.

The brand tenets of honesty and social responsibility influence every business decision they make for customers and employees. The company responds to all emails and addresses customer complaints personally, not with automated messages. When upset customers reached out to Honest Tea about a bottle design change – one done to use less plastic and resin than most bottles – the company replied to all of them personally and explained the environmental benefits of the change, transforming upset customers into delighted ones. And Seth, the company's Tea-EO (CEO), showed how he honestly values employees by finding creative alternatives to layoffs during the recession, as well as offering an employee wellness program that encourages volunteerism and community involvement.

Little Things Mean a Lot: Find Unique Ways to Delight Your Customers

Even the smallest customer interactions are opportunities to solidify your brand in their minds.

Thinking through every touchpoint the customer has with you is a great way to find those tiny moments that can make you "buzz-worthy." Companies that live their brand inside and out do this well.

Customers don't just see your ads, your website, or your office. What if you send them emails? Do you have an interesting email signature that showcases your logo and tagline, along with providing links to promotions or website pages? If you've won any awards, can you tout them in your email signature to reinforce your image as a great company with which to do business? If your brand has a playful attitude, can you word your automated emails in fun, fresh, or irreverent ways?

What about your office phone or customer service lines? How do employees answer the phone? If you run a beauty salon, does your receptionist simply say, "Jennifer speaking," or could she say something like, "This is Jennifer. How can we make you feel fabulous today?" Even your voicemail message can be carefully worded, or you can choose telephone "hold" music that aligns with your brand. I used to love working at Discovery Communications, owners of The Discovery Channel, TLC, Animal Planet, and other great networks. If you called and were placed on hold, you'd enjoy African tribal rhythms or some other world music. This was actually fun for customers and partners, and the music was exactly what you'd expect Discovery to play, in keeping with their brand image. Yes, they could have done nothing and let boring "easy listening" assault your ears, but they chose to use that tiny interaction as a way to further the "Discovery experience." The following Brand at Work case study shows how brand is used to differentiate one business in a lookalike industry, and how Dr. Jaffe conveys her brand through every possible customer touchpoint, great or small.

\\

BRAND AT WORK: LEMON-AID COUNSELING

Psychotherapy is not an industry known for innovative branding, but Dr. Jaelline Jaffe, PhD is out to change that. Practicing since 1976, she started offering an 8-week Lemon-Aid course that utilized her personal experiences overcoming health issues.

Clients connected with the theme, so in 2004 she rebranded her Los Angeles practice as Lemon-Aid Counseling (www.LemonAidCounseling.com) and put up a website. Her mission is to help others develop a positive attitude about their life circumstances, so they can turn their life's lemons into something much sweeter. In a sea of lookalike therapists (especially in L.A.) with predictable business cards and marketing attitudes, she wanted to stand out and attract the right client. Clients who love her brand instantly feel safe, accepted, and positive." Through my branding," she says, "I've created a filter to get responses from those who 'get it' and who connect with my down-to-earth, comforting, optimistic, and genuine style."

Dr. Jaffe lives her brand visually through her website, with its lemon tree graphics and *Make Lemonade* song link, and via her lemon tree business card logo (people at networking events quickly recognize her as The Lemonade Lady). Her office space further conveys the brand, with lemon posters and reproductions of old lemon crate labels, a needle-point pillow (given to her by a client) with the tagline *When life gives you lemons ... make lemonade!,* a lemon-painted lamp, lemon-shaped post-it pads, and lemon To-Do lists for client "homework" reminders. She experientially conveys her brand with a never-ending supply of lemon drops in the waiting room, lemonade and lemon-printed napkins for meetings, and offers client networking gifts like lemon baskets with lemon cookies, shampoos, air fresheners, or lemon cake recipes. And she'll take potential business affiliates to lunch at local area spots like Lemonade, Lemon Moon, or Lemongrass.

To communicate her other brand values of comfort, caring, respect, peace, and a welcoming approach, Dr. Jaffe carefully designed her office and waiting room. Clients are greeted by mellow music, soft colors, low lighting, comfortable furniture, and personalized items (like toys for the kids and magazines for both men and women of all ages). Clients have told her, "I walk into the office and immediately feel held, comforted, and at peace. It's like I can take a deep breath!"

///

Many high-end stores will wrap your purchase in a neat and careful way that's worthy of the price you paid for that merchandise. Some of them take on the extra expense of colored tissue paper to match their visual identity. I remember Victoria's Secret used to wrap purchases in pink or black and white striped paper. It made you feel as though you'd bought yourself a gift. Many stores have specific ways of handling the transaction as well. Nordstrom clerks will never hand you the bag over the cash register like a sack of potatoes. They carefully pack it for you, finish the transaction, and then walk around the counter to hand your bag to you in a poised and civilized way, no matter how busy the store is that day. And many high-end men's stores have a very particular way they show merchandise to customers, gracefully draping the tie over their arm to show you what it looks like instead of holding it up like a dangling wet fish.

These little touches all make sense in the context of the larger Brand Strategy.

Once your strategy is baked, you can find a thousand creative ways to parlay that brand into each and every customer interaction.

And you won't be performing random acts – they will all fit together within the brand promise. This is the little secret that will truly delight your customers.

Many companies with good products or services haven't succeeded in business, but the ones that use brand to surprise and enchant their customers at every turn often create rabid fans. Virgin America Airlines does this very well, conveying their fun, hip, and laid-back style in every detail: soft pink or purple in-cabin lighting; TV's at every seat where you can order food at any time; their cleverly-worded, slightly irreverent gate signage, such as, "While impressive, if your bag is bigger than 24 inches x 16 inches x 10 inches, it must be checked;" and even their in-flight safety video. Rather than a stiff actor giving me the same instructions we've started to tune out on every other flight, Virgin America shows a stylized animated video with all sorts of crazy characters – even a bull calmly reading a magazine next to an anxious bullfighter. The company's sassy, humorous tone carries over to the script as well: "For the 0.0001% of you who've never operated a seat belt before, here's how it works." It's such a simple thing, but is indeed another customer touchpoint they chose to use as a brand opportunity. After all, they want to make flying fun again.

> Small businesses have these same opportunities to be creative, regardless of budget.

Look for those opportunities, however small, and find ways to seal your brand onto the heart of your customers. Best of all, many touches don't need to cost you an additional dime if you can get creative with things you already provide, as we'll see from Red Dingo's story below.

BRAND AT WORK: RED DINGO

Little things do mean a lot – even wording your customer thank you note in an innovative way. Red Dingo (www.reddingo.com) designs and markets pet accessories. That's what they do. What they *are* is a young, progressive company that believes "near enough isn't good enough." When I ordered my Black Lab Eddie's new ID tag, it came in the mail with a card – addressed to Eddie – saying they hoped he enjoyed his new tag, and it would help him find his way back home from all his adventures. They knew that I as a customer cared about my pet, or I wouldn't have ordered this stylish little ID tag. I mean, Eddie didn't pick it out himself. They knew I'd get a kick out of having the card addressed to my dog. It also made me feel like they see my pet as I do: a member of the family. Having a warm, playful brand affected their decisions right down to how my order was packaged and worded. A regular *Thank you for your order* would have been acceptable, but that wasn't good enough for them.

Hire Well: Every New Hire is a Brand Ambassador

I once worked for a large, multinational software company. We had a strong vision and good corporate values and it was a great place to work. But I never quite felt the company's vision and values actually connected to what we did on a daily basis. Many companies face this challenge to apply their guiding principles on a practical level. I didn't think we had a well-defined brand, though all the pieces were there, ripe for a full-blown brand execution. We were well-respected, trustworthy, and our customers loved us.

Then, new marketing leaders came in and tried to move the brand a few steps in the right direction. The advertising became more inspirational, showing people how our software could help them do their jobs better, instead of rattling off a list of features and functions (as every other B2B software company seems to do.) And while this was definitely the right direction, I always felt it wasn't grounded in anything real. The claims weren't grounded in a larger corporate Brand Strategy. Everything came from the marketing department, and we weren't embracing the brand holistically as a company, deep down in our bones. What was finance's role to play in that customer promise? Or engineering? Or even legal?

Then one day I saw an intriguing email go out. It was an internal HTML email from human resources, showcasing all the recruiting sites and activities that their team had implemented. I clicked around on some of these sites meant for outside recruits. They talked about sports teams the company sponsored, community events we supported, and the like. I was floored by the information. First of all, as an employee I didn't know half the things we were sponsoring as a company, yet HR was promoting these activities to people who didn't even work there! I was on the Grant Committee and knew about our own office's amazing community activities, but not the work from other offices and countries. This was all being presented to potential new hires as part of our brand. But I *worked* for the company and didn't even know this was our brand and what we were portraying ourselves to be. It was actually kind of cool: I remember saying, "Wow! This is a company I would totally work for!"

Now, as I said, this was indeed a great company for which to work, but my issue was the fact that HR presented a brand to potential new hires that wasn't quite the reality of working there. And I knew this because I worked there and had experienced none of these things. I thought it was kind of sad that HR had developed a clearer brand for the company than its own marketing team. What amazing things could we have achieved if marketing and HR had been in lockstep on messaging? We could have been attracting more of the right customers and employees to truly live that brand inside and out.

Indeed, brand can be a huge recruitment tool for a company, as was the case with Bakery on Main. In the following Brand at Work case study, the company did a great job of recreating a local bakery experience online, and that strong brand enticed one of their most loyal customer fans to actually seek work at the company.

BRAND AT WORK: BAKERY ON MAIN

Many people love the smells and sights of their local neighborhood bakery. But that experience is different if you have Celiac disease and need to eat gluten-free products that often taste bland and boring. In 2003, Michael Smulders launched Bakery on Main (www.bakeryonmain.com) from the back of his natural foods store to provide tasty, gluten-free granola. People loved it and the company now distributes its delicious products internationally and online. Their mission is to make foods that are good for you but taste like they aren't. While the present focus is on gluten-free granola, they purposefully crafted a company name, logo, and mission to more generally refer to great-tasting natural products of any kind, so the brand can extend to more products in the future.

Trying to capture that small bakery feel, the brand focuses on being homegrown, tasty, casual, local, neighborly, and trustworthy, and only delivering quality products. Even though you can't walk into their store when you buy over the web, the company recently revamped their website with a homey feel to create an online experience that makes you feel like you've walked into the bakery. The striped awnings in their logo and on their new packaging convey a neighborhood feeling, and this consistency creates an instant connection.

The brand attribute of quality is proven through their certifications (recently, the Kosher Parve designation and they are working toward the gluten-free certification) and partnering only with the best suppliers that meet a rigorous selection process and must adhere to strict manufacturing and ingredient standards. This further builds consumer trust. The trustworthy brand attribute comes out on their website, which includes transparent and detailed product ingredient information, full production disclosure and facts about the facility.

Perhaps the best brand compliment? Their marketing associate, Sara Lefebvre, was a loyal customer and jumped at the chance to work there. "I was attracted to their story and their humble beginnings, not to mention the great taste. As someone with Celiac disease, I can identify with our customers and have a unique passion for the company."

///

I'm amazed more businesses don't link up their marketing and HR teams and have them work together. Both groups are responsible for vital internal and external communications that should be aligned.

> The marketing department can spearhead brand-building efforts but they don't *own* brand evangelism: that's everyone's job.

If hiring practices are closely aligned with brand efforts, then the HR team can make better hiring decisions and attract the right kind of people, who will in turn embrace and live out the brand, thus further cementing it externally. And the cycle will continue. But if you don't know your brand well, you can't possibly determine if people will be a good fit for your organization or if their values align with yours. Brand can provide a Litmus test to not only communicate the right things about your company to customers, but also to potential employees – and even partners.

If I'd followed my own advice, I'd have seen a red flag waving a mile away when I interviewed with a technology start-up firm ten years ago. In my interview with the product marketing manager, I asked, "What kind of culture would you say you have here?"

His answer was, "We don't really have a culture, but that's why we need a strong marketing director. Marketing can create one for us."

Wow. I should have run away right then and there. Marketing can craft and shepherd the right brand, based on market demand, competitive analysis, and customer feedback. It's their job to take all of that information, synthesize it, and then figure out the best way to convey the right image and messages to the world in order to attract more sales and customers. And yes, it can even inform internal processes and policies if there is executive sponsorship from the top.

But marketing cannot bear the sole responsibility of forcing a culture or brand on a company. If, as I've said throughout this book, brand is part of everything and every interaction, then every employee has a role to play in fulfilling that brand promise. So they have to know what it is, embrace it, understand it, and contribute to it. I believe great brand adoption starts at the top and rolls downhill. If the founder or CEO commits to a strong brand vision, verbalized and perfected by the marketing team in many cases, the rest of the company will fall in line. But if the person at the top doesn't think brand is important and isn't creating a mission-based organization, then the true assets of that organization – the people – will reflect that attitude as well.

Josh Levine of Great Monday (www.great-monday. com) calls this *culture-driven branding*. "Programs that have the most effect are the ones that engage people within the company. It's all about culture – the sum of the decisions that any one person or group makes," says Josh.

How do you engage your people to understand and make better decisions about what they're doing day in and day out? Josh says if you can teach your employees the company values, they will make better decisions on how that brand is expressed in their jobs. "Your people are making decisions time and time again, and a company's money will be much better spent if it's able to create and invest in a brand education program that propagates itself." If your people know why they are coming to work, they can align to your mission and help you achieve it. Give them a purpose and control over their destiny.

That's the amazing opportunity available to entrepreneurs, small business CEO's, and start-up firms. You are young and you are nimble. You're closer to your customers and employees than large corporations. You have the power to create a brand as amazingly sticky as Apple, Nike, or Virgin if you want. But your Brand Strategy needs to start at the top and permeate not just advertising and marketing, but hiring, operations, customer care, finance, production, and every other aspect of your company. It can help determine the right people to bring into the organization and ensure they'll be ambassadors for your brand.

When to Rebrand

Rebranding can mean overhauling your visual look and feel, or even updating your core messages to adapt to changing needs, different competitors, a new market, or customer feedback. It means you're making a new promise to your target audience and you need to communicate that difference in everything you do. We may only take notice of visual rebranding efforts because they're most apparent. But brands can and should evolve, even if their core mission remains the same. Most companies will stay true at their core to the mission-based brand promise they offer, in terms of their operations, product quality, and ideal customer, but they try to update their look, tweak their messaging, or change distribution decisions to adapt to changing tastes and needs.

My favorite example of this is a story from Guy Kawasaki's book, *Rules for Revolutionaries* (Harper Collins, 1999). His story wasn't framed in the context of rebranding, but it's a great example of retooling your message to fit market needs. In 1886, a woman named Josephine Cochrane invented the dishwasher. She didn't do this to save time and effort, as she had many servants who performed these tasks for her. But her servants broke too many dishes cleaning them manually so she invented the dishwasher to save her china. This helped her sell her product to hotels and restaurants – but not to homeowners. Why? Homeowners didn't consider washing dishes a hard task. So she tweaked her message to focus on the dishwasher's ability to sterilize the dishes in extremely hot water and keep your family healthier. The brand's benefit was changed to focus on "better health" rather than "saving time" for that audience.

While you don't want to change your brand every six months, some reasons to rebrand could include:

- Your colors and imagery are dated (i.e., you will be viewed as behind the times and irrelevant)
- You are now targeting a different buyer (i.e, you used to sell only to women and now want to attract more men; you used to sell to low-level analysts and you now sell to C-level execs)
- Your offerings or price points have changed (i.e, from a cheap technology tool to an expensive solution suite)
- You have direct feedback that your brand is repelling your target customer or is being completely misinterpreted (this one takes time to assess)
- Your competition has changed (i.e., more competitors have swarmed the market and all of you look and sound the same)

Another big reason companies rebrand is due to a merger, acquisition, or change in positioning. Monster.com was a client of mine when I worked for Young & Laramore, a Midwestern ad agency, back in 1998-1999. Initially, our client had been Online Career Center (OCC), another online job posting site. In 1999, the Monster Board (as it was known pre-merger) merged with OCC, because OCC was well-known and respected among HR professionals – the ones paying for the ads. This was a symbiotic deal. The combined company rebranded as Monster.com and revamped their look, feel, and messaging in advance of the big launch.

At the same time, Monster.com needed to relaunch within the HR community to tout that OCC was now Monster.com and to unveil new online features and offerings. They needed HR professionals to start seeing Monster.com in a different light then they'd viewed The Monster Board. The former brand image among hiring managers and recruiters was that The Monster Board only attracted young, inexperienced job seekers, or worse, those who couldn't find a job anywhere else. Old brand perceptions die hard: Monster.com had to shift those mental perceptions – not just change their look and feel.

At the time, online job boards were new and Internet usage wasn't as pervasive as it is today. Many recruiters were still spending money on newspaper classified ads and not investing heavily in online methods. So the brand positioning had to compete with not only other online job boards as competitors but primarily with traditional media.

Formerly, the company put heavy emphasis on resume quantity instead on quality. Their name – The Monster Board – emphasized huge numbers of resumes, not quality candidates. No one had more resumes or job seekers, their positioning screamed. All of their benefits focused on "more, more, more." Now, with this newly combined company, they had to create a more differentiated message to entice both job seekers and recruiters and address different needs.

Our agency dealt with the HR positioning. But we saw how both the recruiter and the job seeker positioning were inextricably linked: if you didn't feed the engine with qualified candidates, then you wouldn't attract more recruiters. And if you didn't have good recruiters posting on the site, you'd never attract the caliber of job seeker they wanted. The promises to each audience had to be delivered at the same time.

After interviews and focus groups with HR managers, we found the online benefit of quantity was important, but it also produced a new need: filtering resumes. Soon, *quality* started to trump *quantity*. They were less concerned with seeing hundreds of resumes than they were with finding one *perfect* resume. There was one job to fill and only one person needed to fill it. The rest was just clutter. This was in the day before niche and industry-specific job posting sites, which solved many of these problems. So we focused the ad campaign positioning on quality, not quantity. Yes, it was true that with more "crop" you tend to find more "cream" (one of our ad headlines) but that assumed there was quality in that crop to begin with.

We created a strategic position that focused on Monster. com as the best source for passive job seekers: those who were valuable and still employed, but might be lured away by the right opportunity. A recruiter always loves to find someone *before* they're starting a job search. The brand positioning shifted to convince HR execs that Monster.com didn't attract the desperately unemployed, but attracted those who were currently employed and might be open to a better opportunity. After all, everyone in any job has a bad day or dreams of career improvement. These more desirable candidates weren't actively looking, but could be convinced it was safe to look. We called these people "the vaguely dissatisfied." In this way, recruiters could get in front of quality candidates and find the perfect one.

On the other side of the funnel, the job seeker messaging focused on quality as well – quality as it pertained to finding the perfect job. Monster.com wasn't about having the most jobs, but about finding a job that fit your aspirations and passions. That message was captured in their famous "When I Grow Up" 1999 Super Bowl ad, created by the company's Massachusetts-based consumer ad agency, Mullen. The humorous black-and-white ad featured a series of hopeful children saying things like, "When I grow up ... I want to be ...a yes-man," "...to have a brown nose" and " ...to be forced into early retirement." The message wasn't merely, "Find a job at Monster.com" but "Find a *better* job at Monster. com."

This quality-of-life messaging worked to get more job seekers onto the site, which satisfied the needs of all those new recruiters we were attracting on our end through print and online ads. Job searches per minute, a crucial measurement for them, spiked post-Super Bowl and remained high for days afterward.[12]

Often a company may need to rebrand – or create an entirely new brand – when they find a new use for their products or a new audience that demands what they offer. Such was the case when Edward Mirell spun its brand off from its parent company to carve out an entirely new market they could lead.

---

[12] Paul McNamara, *Monster.com's Super Bowl Ads Pay Off in a Big Way,* http://www.cnn.com (February 8, 1999)

BRAND AT WORK: EDWARD MIRELL

How can you "grow" a brand to serve a completely different market? When your market is crowded, you often have to forge a new category that plays to your strengths so you can be heard above the crowd. Edward Mirell (www. edwardmirell.com) leveraged its experience in innovative design, manufacturing, and marketing to establish itself as the recognized leader of a new jewelry category.

Edward Mirell's parent company is Spectore Corporation, which spent years of research in titanium development with a singular focus on titanium's applications for consumer products. "As our pallet of materials and technologies grew, so did the number of inquiries from and orders from many of the world's leading brands. In 2004 we decided it was time for us to apply our vast and uniquely diverse resources in design, development, and manufacturing expertise into a signature brand: Edward Mirell," says Edward Rosenberg, Designer and CEO. Edward Mirell is a privately-held design jewelry brand focused on using contemporary metals, like titanium, and cutting edge technology to break new ground in fashion.

Their brand oozes boldness, edginess, innovation, and exceptional quality. You can see this in their website: a modern, elegant look of bold blacks and grays. Their copy expertly uses all the right words to craft their story. The tone is aspirational, epic and carries exactly the right sense of high-end "coolness" – minus any pretension. Even their sales portfolio consistently conveys this high-end vibe.

By their very nature, these products appeal to people who want something different – and diversity is key to their brand success. "We clearly recognize that our lofty goal involves clearly defining difference at every turn. So we approach every initiative by exploring the broadest possible diversity in design, process, display, and marketing. For example, only a small percentage of the design and development teams in our jewelry division come from the jewelry world. We have graphic designers, animators, illustrators, sculptors, fashion designers, engineers, architects, and industrial designers all working together. Viva la difference."

Edward knows a differentiated brand cannot be successful if it tries to please everyone. Their pieces tend to appeal to tech communities and alternative lifestyle groups. Edward Mirell's target consumer is fashion-forward and career-driven with a passion for excitement and travel. Typically of Generations X or Y, they follow the latest trends and are brand-conscious while seeking value and quality in the items they purchase. They are educated; therefore, they research and understand style innovations, the latest materials and intricacies, or quality in design. The proof is in numerous design awards, world-reknowned partner organizations, a loyal fan base and many celebrity devotees.

You can see there's an important time and place for rebranding, but this doesn't mean you should do it all the time. It is easy to get scared and second-guess yourself with branding as you see more innovative and creative options out there. If you consistently communicate a clear brand and you know you're tapping into the right needs for your audience, then you shouldn't worry. Good designers keep changing styles in mind when creating your visual identity. They should avoid colors or designs that are too trendy and become outdated in a year.

However, if your brand is about being on the cutting edge and being modern, this can be a fine line to walk. You should be able to maintain whatever you select for at least a few years, not only to keep your costs down in changing everything out, but to ensure the brand gains momentum with people. While you may be sick of your branding after six months, many of your ideal customers will only have interacted with it once or twice. They haven't had a chance to form a connection yet. Nike started with their "swoosh" many years ago and now it comes to symbolize their brand promise, given the amount of time and money they've put into it. The company's brand promise has evolved over time, but it remains true to the core of what they deliver. That has never changed.

You may find you need to update the look and feel of your brand eventually to stand out from what is now a crowded marketplace or to inject new life into the brand. Rebranding can be a great way to build buzz again and shake up customer apathy. But be careful how you do this.

Scott Montgomery states, "Updating branding is one of the precious few controls a marketer has to create 'energy' and 'news' around an established brand. But it has to be more than just a logical, clever and systematic undertaking. Will change enhance the story the brand embodies without losing sight of its history?"

Understanding your Brand Strategy – your core reason for being – intimately and staying tuned to why customers buy from you at both a conscious and subconscious level can help you avoid such slip-ups when it comes time to update your look.

Everything Stems From Brand

The right Brand Strategy is the core to building a strong organization. The brand may indeed evolve over time, but it's important to think about your reason for being, your ideal customers, and your corporate personality before you embark on building a website, a logo or any of the other visual representations of brand. Consult your brand before you create corporate messaging or put any marketing programs in place. Otherwise, you'll waste time and money and not grow your business at all.

Your Brand Strategy serves as the guidepost to all your business decisions, from which marketing tactics to employ, to how to decorate your store, to what colors and font to use on your website, to the type of people you hire. If you can't believe in and articulate your brand, then no one else will. Brand can inform your operations inside and out to give customers a more consistent experience. And while your brand ultimately lives in the minds of customers, you can influence those perceptions and attitudes with many tools that are within your control.

A Brand Strategy will give you a host of benefits as you move forward. You'll be able to define who you are and who you serve, crisply and cleanly. You can more efficiently spread the word about what you do by pairing the right messages with the right tactics. You will focus on only the most effective channels to reach your target audience. You can tailor messaging for different audiences that contains a unified mission and vision. And tactically, you'll save time and money on design, writing, and promotion.

You might be small, but you can think big.

Use brand as the opportunity to create a mission-driven organization that adds something to the world and to the lives of those you touch: customers, employees, partners and even the community at large. Who knows? Maybe someday, someone will tattoo *your* logo onto their arm with pride.

About the Author

Maria Ross is a brand strategist, writer, and speaker who helps entrepreneurs, small to midsize businesses, and fast-growth companies engage, inform, and delight their customers. She owns Red Slice, a consultancy that offers brand and messaging strategy and workshops to clients all over the world. Previously, she was a Silicon Valley marketing executive, creating winning strategies for start-ups and multinational technology companies.

With almost 20 years of experience on both the client and agency sides, Maria has worked with the likes of Discovery Networks, Microsoft, Monster.com, Accenture, and Business Objects (an SAP company). In addition, she has volunteered her brand expertise pro-bono to non-profits and is a sought-after speaker for conferences and workshops. Maria has appeared in Entrepreneur Magazine, Seattle Business, Columbus CEO, The Los Angeles Times, American Express OPEN Forum, and WomenEntrepreneur.com

Maria is also an actress and published food and wine writer who lives with her husband, Paul and their black Lab, Eddie, in Seattle, Washington.

For wise perspectives and winsome wit, please visit Maria's blog at www.red-slice.com. You can also contact and learn more from Maria by joining her Twitter battalion @ RedSlice or becoming a fan at www.facebook.com/RedSlice.

Acknowledgements

A big thank you to Dee and Sammie Justesen and Nadene Carter at NorLightsPress for making this book a reality. You never forget your big break, and their support has been incredible.

I wouldn't be writing today without the support of my amazing family. Thanks to Mom and Dad Piccininni and Patrick, John, and Michael who have encouraged (or patiently tolerated?) my writing, musings, and opinions since the tender age of five. Thanks also to Anita, Lori, and Val and the DeMauro and Ross families for their cheerleading.

Thanks to my "writing divas," Whitney Keyes and Elisabeth Dale. You gals kept my momentum going with your ideas and advice. For research, a big thanks to Carlie Hanson, a gutsy gal with enthusiasm to spare. And thanks to Sarah Wilson, Outspoken Media, Karen Rosenzweig, Betsy Talbot, Emilia Skrinar and Lucia Carruthers for helping with publicity.

Many mentors have contributed – whether they know it or not – to my branding philosophies and education. I thank them from the bottom of my inquisitive heart.

Thanks to Scott Montgomery and Mark Bradley for the wonderful branding work they put out into the world and for balancing artistic integrity with business reality (very rare indeed). Years ago, you welcomed me over from the "big bad Account Management side" of our ad agency and patiently answered my every question as I sought to learn more about the magic you do. Thanks to Carrie Voorhis, a gifted writer who teaches me about the power of words to move people; to Marty Neumeier, a brand guru I admire for his brilliant simplicity; and to Kathi Kaplan, Caroline Waterson, and Susan Marfise who taught me the power of marketing planning and how "fewer activities done the right way" will actually yield greater success. Thanks to Patrick Morrissey, Guy Weismantel, and Lance Walter – master storytellers who bring brand personality to an often bland industry; to Melody Biringer, entrepreneur extraordinaire, for being a constant inspiration and good friend; to Bridget Perez, Isabelle Englund-Geiger, and Scott Lawrence for their tremendous design and digital abilities grounded in brand truths. Special thanks to Bridget for this book's cover design.

Thank you to my big brand heroes like Nike, Apple, Starbucks, and Virgin for having the courage and commitment to connect on a visceral level with your customers. I learn more from you all the time. And thank you to all the amazing small businesses I profiled, as well as all of Red Slice's clients. Your desire to create something better in the world inspires me no end.

Most importantly, thanks to Paul, my husband and friend, who not only constantly teaches me about product marketing and messaging, but who adores me, encourages me, and paves the way to making everything possible while encouraging all my crazy ideas. Love you.

Available from NorlightsPress and
fine booksellers everywhere

Toll free: 888-558-4354   **Online:** www.norlightspress.com
Shipping Info: Add $2.95 - first item and $1.00 for each additional item

Name _____

Address _____

Daytime Phone _____

E-mail _____

No. Copies	Title	Price (each)	Total Cost

	Subtotal	
	Shipping	
	Total	

Payment by (circle one):
   Check   Visa   Mastercard   Discover   Am Express

Card number_____3 digit code_____

Exp.date_____ Signature_____

Mailing Address:
762 State Road 458
Bedford IN 47421

Sign up to receive our catalogue at
www.norlightspress.com

Made in the USA
Lexington, KY
07 July 2013